Starter

Student Book

Ben Wetz

OXFORD

UNIVERSITY PRESS

Reading and Listening	Speaking and Functions	Writing	Pronunciation and Study skills
• Classmates • Clubs • Answers please!	• Giving personal information	• An e-mail message: capital letters	• Counting syllables • Guessing the meanings of words
• Faces • Collectors • Actors	• Describing an actor • Asking about possessions • Asking about a diary	• A personal description: using notes	• Word stress (1)

• Culture File: Families in the U.S. and the U.K.   • World of Pop 1: Britney Spears, *Lucky*

• Diets • Healthy habits • Brains	• Talking about likes and dislikes • Asking about habits	• Lifestyles: *and* and *but*	• Third person -s: /ɪz/, /s/, and /z/ • Remembering vocabulary
• Playing the game • Big star • No limits	• Talking about habits and routines • Talking about sports activities	• A perfect day: *first, next, after that,* and *finally*	• /h/

• Culture File: National sports – baseball, soccer, and ice hockey   • World of Pop 2: Vanessa Amorosi, *Absolutely Everybody*

• Photo album • Carnival • Special days	• Describing people in a picture	• Description of a festival: planning a paragraph	• -*ing* forms • Using a dictionary
• Trans-Sahara • Traffic and transportation • School trip	• Asking for things in a store • Asking about places in a town	• An informal letter	• /s/ + consonant

• Culture File: Clubs for young people   • World of Pop 3: Gloria Estefan, *You'll be mine*

• Skills • Danger! • Wild!	• Asking about abilities	• Description of an animal: planning an essay	• Weak forms: *can* • Finding information
• Paint and decorate • Neighbors • Mystery house	• Talking about plans for decorating a classroom • Giving opinions about computer games	• Giving reasons: *because*	• /ɪ/ and /i/

• Culture File: Going out and staying in   • World of Pop 4: Enrique Iglesias, *Be with you*

• Famous names • Fame and fortune • Superstars	• Talking about a movie	• A biography: sequencing	• Simple past -*ed*: /ɪd/ • Word building
• Space Camp® • On the moon • Contact	• Asking about a vacation	• A story: checking spelling	• Word stress (2)

• Culture File: A visitor's view of the U.S. and the U.K.   • World of Pop 5: Robbie Williams, *She's the one*

OXFORD
UNIVERSITY PRESS

Great Clarendon Street, Oxford OX2 6DP

Oxford University Press is a department of the University of Oxford.
It furthers the University's objective of excellence in research, scholarship,
and education by publishing worldwide in

Oxford New York

Auckland Cape Town Dar es Salaam Hong Kong Karachi
Kuala Lumpur Madrid Melbourne Mexico City Nairobi
New Delhi Shanghai Taipei Toronto

With offices in

Argentina Austria Brazil Chile Czech Republic France Greece
Guatemala Hungary Italy Japan Poland Portugal Singapore
South Korea Switzerland Thailand Turkey Ukraine Vietnam

OXFORD and OXFORD ENGLISH are registered trade marks of
Oxford University Press in the UK and in certain other countries

© Oxford University Press 2007

The moral rights of the author have been asserted

Database right Oxford University Press (maker)

First published 2007

2011 2010 2009 2008 2007

10 9 8 7 6 5 4 3 2 1

ISBN: 978 0 19 452700 2

Printed in China

ACKNOWLEDGEMENTS

*The Publishers and author would like to thank the following teachers for their help in
developing the course*: Angelica Puelles, Luciana Hernández, María Cecilia
Shecre, Silvia Stagnaro, Corina Arguimbau, Fabiana Siciliano, Silvia Luppi,
Graciela Beatriz Salinas, María Amelia Alexandre de Cetro, María Beatriz de
Benedet, Paola Santanera, Susana Elsa Sainz, María Laura Provvisionato,
Viviana Ameijenda, Vanessa Schwarzbach, Virginia Lorena Alvarez, Juana
Nicenboim, Adriana Toniolli, Alejandra Rouzeaut, Lorena Mollini, Verónica
de la Encina, María Celia Baez, María del Rosario González, Pierina Gatani,
Patricia Arriondo, Andriana Gil, Elizabeth Felix, Daniela Oliveira Guerra,
Debora Schisler, Elisabeth Moreira S. Silva, Flavia Moreira Landucci, Sonia
Maria Proença Cury, Nilce Chaud Albano, Patricia Rossi Julio, Fife MacDuff,
Maria Zita Bierrench, Helena Gordon, Beth Rodrigues Roselli, Mária Lucia
Gallina, Beatriz de Farias, Maria de Lourdes Genestreti, Margareth Perucci,
Maria Alice Gonçalves Antunes

Illustrations by: Arlene Adams pp 26, 48, 58, 70, 75 (signs), 81, 92, 114; Nila Aye/
New Division pp 34 (objects), 77 (objects), 78 (butterflies), 100; Kathy Baxendale
p 77 (fish); Adrian Barclay pp 37, 42 (football, racquet); Jonas Bergstrand pp 31
(TV), 64 (weather), 75 (boots, backpack), 85; Brett Breckon pp 71, 74, 78 (needle
etc); Chris Brown p 72; Nick Duffy pp 61, 105 (planet); Andrew Foley/Eastwing
p 12 (people); Simon Gurr pp 12 (objects), 42 (bike etc); Andre Labrie pp 31
(comics), 73; Bill Ledger pp 34 (musical indigestion), 64 (cartoon strip), 97,
108; Andrew Parker p 84; Andrew Peters pp 15, 20 (Wanted), 106; Simeon
Stout pp 12 (cartoon strip), 20 (friends), 105 (cartoon strip); Anthony Williams
pp 52, 53, 82, 83; Richard Williams/Eastwing pp 17, 29, 56, 64 (objects)

We would also like to thank the following for the permission to reproduce photographs:
Action Images p 47 (ice hockey), Action Plus p 40 (sand skiing); Agencia Cover
pp 23 (model), 99; Alamy p 36 (basketball hoop), 45 (baseball souvenirs), 67
(club), 113 (Scottish countryside); Allsport pp 38, 43 (football); Emily Andersen
pp 6, 7, 18, 21 (group), 22, 23 (group), 28 (two couples), 34, 36 (people), 41
(girl), 43 (shopping), 44, 45 (shopping), 50 (Scotland x 2), 54 (New Year's Eve),
59, 60 (train), 65 (computer), 66, 67 (computer), 87 (couple), 88, 89 (reading,
computer), 109 (cooking), 110, 111; Aquarius p 94 (Harry Potter/Johnny Depp),
Steve Betts pp 16, 20, 45 (objects), 50 (Brazilians), 62 (sad girl), 67, 80, 113
(shopping); Boy Scouts of America pp 65, 68; Bridgeman Art Library p 93
(Beethoven); Bruce Coleman Collection p 76 (eagle); Bubbles Photolibrary
pp 33 (Pauline Cutler), 67 (two girls in street), 89 (sad girl); Lars Carlsson p 14;
Collections pp 96 (Beatles), 46 (football crowd); Corbis pp 13 (Johnny Depp/
Scarlett Johansson), 15 (Keira Knightley), 19 (Orlando Bloom), 30 (grandfather
playing computer game), 39, 86 (books), 90 (reading), 91 (centre & left), 94,
(Beethoven, Bach); Corbisstockmarket p 89 (meeting); James Davis p 63 (safari);
Ecoscene p 113 (animal rights); EMPICS Sports Photo Agency p 10 (Olympic
flag); Eye Ubiquitous pp 35 (swimmer, hockey), 60 (school bus), 72 (boy);
Fortean Picture Library p 106; Frank Spooner Pictures p 94 (Salvador Dali);
Getty Images pp 5, 6 (US Teen girls), 7 (Jessica), 10 (desert), 11, 23 (Jessica
Alba/Raica Oliveira), 28 (curry), 29, 32 (brain), 35 (basketball, football, table
tennis, volleyball, skiing), 40 (kayaking, snowboarding), 41 (crowd, football),
45 (baseball card/ baseball team as part of composite), 46 (baseball), 49 (New
Year, Easter), 50 (Kenya x 2), 54 (Vatican, Mexico), 55, 57 (rain, sun, wet, hot),
60 (car, plane, bicycle, motorbike), 62 (cyclist), 63 (skiing), 67 (teen boy
looking at watch), 69 (dancing, snack bar), 72 (old man), 76 (camels,
chameleon), 78, 81, 85 (PhotoDisc), 86 (lampshade, desk), 93 (Cafu, Giselle),
104 (Woman),107, 112 (cars in snow/ girls in car); Greg Evans International
pp 21 (Britney Spears), 26, 109 (Times Square, Piccadilly Circus); Idols pp 43
(Vanessa Amorossi), 48 (Vanessa Amorossi), 94 (Destiny's child), 99 (Robbie
Williams); Image State pp 10 (chip), 57 (cloud, wind); Impact Photos p 47
(baseball); John Birdsall Social Issues Photo Library p 112 (bus queue); John
Walmsley Photo Library p 69 (computer lesson); Chris King p 79; Kobal
Collection p 93 (Antonio Banderas); London Features International pp 19
(Cameron Diaz), 114; Lonely planet p 49 (carnival); Magnum Photos p 112
(pudding/Martin Parr); Mall of America pp 87, 91 (right); Mary Evans Picture
Library p 94 (Alexander Graham Bell); MaxPower Aerospace p 86 (converted
plane); Moviestore p 101 (Enemy Mine); NHPA pp 10 (chameleon), 77, 101
(sun, stars); OUP p 35 (tennis) 36 (teen boy), 49 (Thanksgiving), 67 (two girls
on phone), 95 (teen boy and girl), 113 (Fish and chips); Performing Arts Library
p 10 (tango); Pictor International pp 47 (coach), 49 (Christmas), 54 (Chinese
New Year), 90 (shopping); Photofusion p 69 (steel band/Paul Doyle, smiling
girl/Christa Stadtler); Popperfoto p 93 (Albert Einstein); Powerstock/Superstock
pp 10 (White House), 28 (burger), 35 (cycling), 42, 49 (birthday), 57 (cold, dry),
60 (helicopter), 65 (Gloria Estefan), 70, 76 (penguin), 96 (Bill Gates, Michael
Owen); Punchstocks p 7 (teen girls); Retna pictures pp 28 (family), 90 (TV
zapping/Phillip Reeson), 94 (Gladiator, Michael Johnson), 103; Rex Features
pp 15 (Peter Macdairmid), 23 (Fonseca/Justin Timberlake), 24 (Royal Family/
Stewart Mark), 60 (bus), 63 (Disney World/Andy Itkoff), 87, 92 (Enrique Iglesias),
89 (sick girl), 93 (Juan Veron, Salvador Dali), 96 (Pablo Picasso), 96 (Angelina
Jolie), 98 (Christina Aguilera), 99 (Chayanne), 100 (Madonna), 114 (Robbie
Williams); Ronald Grant Archive p 94 (Dracula); Sally & Richard Greenhill
p 112 (street clothes); SPL p 101 (astronauts, UFO, space station, alien, moon,
moon buggy); Charles Seifried p 102 (space camp);Stockbyte p 27 (juice, coffee,
pie); Trip/Art Directors pp 28 (pasta, pizza, cake); 32 (doctor), 49 (Halloween),
50 (Carnival), 86 (cupboard, bed), 104 (man on moon); Topham/Picturepoint
pp 95 (John Lennon), 96 (Gisele Bundchen); Universal Pictorial Press Agency
p 24 (Simpsons)

Commissioned photography by: Emily Andersen, Steve Betts and Chris King

1 ○ Class!

Take a look!

Find the pages where you:
- read about students around the world.
- do a quiz on school subjects.
- write an e-mail message.

Vocabulary

School subjects

1 Match pictures 1–5 with five school subjects in the box.

> ~~ICT~~   history   English   math   music
> P.E.   science   geography   art   French

1 ICT

2 🎧 Listen and repeat the words in exercise 1.

3 What are your favorite subjects?

● VOCABULARY • PAGE 125

1a Classmates

Reading

1 🎧 Read and listen.

The United States

My name's Jessica and I'm thirteen years old. School's OK. This is my classmate, Rachel. She's very good at art and ICT.

Japan

Hello. I'm Tomoko. In this photo, I'm with my friend Chikako. We're in a calligraphy class. Calligraphy is an important subject in Japan.

English
math
science
history
geography

Argentina

Hello. My name's Daniel. In this photo, I'm with my English teacher, Claudia. I'm good at English, but my favorite subject is music.

Australia

Hi, I'm Nick. I'm from Brisbane, Australia. My favorite subject is geography. These are my best friends, Scott and Linda. They're in the school band.

2 Read the texts again. Are the sentences true or false?

Jessica is fourteen. *False.*

1 Rachel is good at art.
2 Chikako is from Japan.
3 Daniel's favorite subject is English.
4 Claudia is a science teacher.
5 Nick and Scott are friends.
6 Linda is from the U.K.

Look!

Demonstrative pronouns

This is my classmate.

These are my best friends.

⬤ GRAMMAR · PAGE 115

Exploring grammar

be: affirmative and negative

3 **Complete the sentences in the grammar chart.**

Affirmative	Negative
I'm twelve.	**I'm not** fourteen.
(1) ...... from Japan.	You **aren't** from Brazil.
He**'s** good at art.	He (2) ...... good at math.
She**'s** a teacher.	She **isn't** a teacher.
It**'s** important.	It (3) ...... important.
(4) ...... in class.	We **aren't** in class.
(5) ...... my friends.	They **aren't** my friends.

GRAMMAR · PAGE 115

4 **Complete the sentences about the texts on page 6. Use *'s*, *'re*, *isn't*, or *aren't*.**

Calligraphy *isn't* a school subject in the U.S.

1 Jessica is thirteen. She ...... from the U.S. She ...... from Britain. She ...... with Rachel in this photo.

2 Tomoko and Chikako ...... from Australia. They ...... from Japan.

3 Daniel ...... with his English teacher. He ...... good at English, but it ...... his favorite subject.

4 This ...... a photo of Scott and Linda. They ...... good at music.

5 **Complete the sentences with the correct form of the verb and your information.**

My name*'s Carlos*.

1 My family name ......
2 My favorite subjects ......
3 I ...... not very good at ......
4 My best friends ....
5 We ...... from ......
6 My teacher ...... from ......
7 English ...... an important subject.
8 I .... years old.

Speaking

6 **In pairs, compare your answers to exercise 5.**

Subject pronouns

7 **Look at the texts on page 6 and complete the chart.**

Singular	Plural
I	(1) ....
you	(2) ....
he / she / it	(3) ....

GRAMMAR · PAGE 115

8 **Complete the sentences with pronouns.**

Help me! *You*'re good at English.

1 Nick is Australian. ......'s from Brisbane.
2 This is my teacher. ......'s called Claudia.
3 Scott and I like music. ......'re in the school band.
4 I like art. ......'s my favorite subject.
5 These are my friends. ......'re in my class.

Finished?

Who are your teachers?
My math teacher is ...

Vocabulary

Interests

1 🎧 Read the notices. Put the letters in order to make the names of six clubs. Then listen and repeat.

nonevritmen – *environment*

1 boricase

2 crotpume

3 hotpoghyrap

4 raketa

5 sicum

6 shecs

◯ **VOCABULARY • PAGE 125**

Reading

2 **Read the notices and answer the questions.**

Where is the environment club?

Room 8.

1 What is the name of the photography club?

2 Who is the karate teacher?

3 What days are the aerobics classes?

4 What time is the computer club?

5 Is the chess club for expert players?

6 Who is the music teacher?

Elm Street School Clubs

The **environment club**

Are you interested in the environment?

Tuesdays 4:15 Room 8

The chess club
Beginners welcome!
Room 4.
Tuesdays and Fridays 4:00

Aerobics

Music and movement
Join us in the gym.

Mondays and Fridays
4:30

Are you crazy about music? ♪

Piano, guitar, flute, and clarinet
classes for all levels

Contact Mrs. Ross

Karate Club

Gym. Wednesday 4:00
Contact Mr. Lamb

Images
The Elm Street photography club

Meetings on Mondays after school

Computer club

Beginners and experts welcome.

Information Technology room
Every day @ 4:20

Listening

3 🎧 Ashley and Mandy are talking about the clubs. Listen and choose the correct answers.

"Are you in a club, Mandy?"

a "Yes, I am." **b** "No, I'm not."

1 "Is Jennifer interested in the environment?"

   a "Yes, she is." **b** "No, she isn't."

2 "Are the karate classes good?"

   a "Yes, they are." **b** "No, they aren't."

3 "Is Mr. Lamb a karate expert?"

   a "Yes, he is." **b** "No, he isn't."

4 "Is the English exam today?"

   a "Yes, it is." **b** "No, it isn't."

Exploring grammar

be: questions

4 Look at the examples in exercise 3. Complete the chart with *is* and *are*.

Am	I	
(1)	you	in room 4?
(2)	he / she / it	
Are	we	
(3)	you	late?
(4)	they	

⬤ **GRAMMAR · PAGE 115**

5 Copy the questions. Write affirmative and negative short answers.

   Are you good at chemistry?

   Yes, I am. / No, I'm not.

1 Are they in the chess club?

2 Is she a computer expert?

3 Is he good at photography?

4 Is it three o'clock?

Speaking

6 Work in pairs. Ask and answer questions.

   A: Are you good at math?

   B: Yes, I am.

1 ...... English classes difficult?

2 ...... it Monday today?

3 ...... your mom interested in photography?

4 ...... your friends interested in sports?

5 ...... you a computer expert?

6 ...... P.E. your favorite subject?

Interrogative pronouns

7 Complete the questions with the pronouns in the box.

How	Where	What time
What	When	Who

   "*How* old are you?" "I'm twelve."

1 "...... are you?" "I'm fine, thanks."

2 "...... is it?" "It's two o'clock."

3 "...... is your math teacher?" "Mr. Evans."

4 "...... is aerobics?" "In the gym."

5 "...... is the exam?" "On Wednesday."

6 "...... is your favorite subject?" "Art."

⬤ **GRAMMAR · PAGE 116**

⬤ **Finished?**

Make a notice for a school club.

Study skills

Guessing the meanings of words

Some words are similar in English and your language.

1 Guess the meanings of words 1–4. Use the pictures in the "Subjects quiz".

1	trumpet	3	the Olympic Games
2	deserts	4	kilobyte

2 Work in pairs. Compare your answers to exercise 1.

3 Find words 1–4 in the quiz. Guess and then check their meanings.

1	instrument	3	mystery
2	microscope	4	taekwondo

● **VOCABULARY • PAGE 125**

Reading

4 Work in pairs. Do the quiz.

SUBJECTS QUIZ

MUSIC

1 What is this instrument?
- **a** A trumpet.
- **b** A saxophone.

2 Where is tango music from?
- **a** Argentina.
- **b** Brazil.

SCIENCE

5 What is this animal?
- **a** A chameleon.
- **b** A dragon.

6 What is this instrument?
- **a** A microscope.
- **b** A telescope.

SPORT

9 What country is taekwondo from?
- **a** Japan.
- **b** Korea.

10 When are the Olympic Games?
- **a** Every three years.
- **b** Every four years.

GEOGRAPHY

3 Where are the Sahara and Kalahari deserts?
- **a** In Australia.
- **b** In Africa.

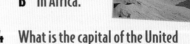

4 What is the capital of the United States?
- **a** New York.
- **b** Washington.

MATH

7 What is the mystery number (?) ?
- **a** 8.
- **b** 6.

`1, 2, 4, ?, 16, 32`

8 What is the mystery number (?) ?
- **a** 22.
- **b** 21.

`1, 2, 4, 7, 11, 16, ?`

ICT

11 What is a kilobyte?
- **a** 1,000 bytes.
- **b** 10,000 bytes.

12 What country is this website from?
- **a** The United Kingdom.
- **b** The United States.

Back Forward Stop Refresh Home Aut

Address @ http://www.oup.co.uk/

Writing

An e-mail message: capital letters

5 Read the e-mail message from Clara and write a reply. Change the red words.

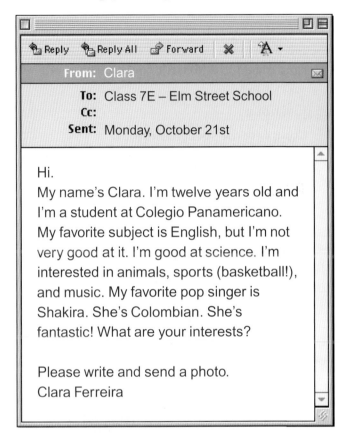

🔄 Reply 🔄 Reply All ➡ Forward ✖ ᴬ ▾

From: Clara ✉

To: Class 7E – Elm Street School
Cc:
Sent: Monday, October 21st

Hi.
My name's Clara. I'm twelve years old and I'm a student at Colegio Panamericano. My favorite subject is English, but I'm not very good at it. I'm good at science. I'm interested in animals, sports (basketball!), and music. My favorite pop singer is Shakira. She's Colombian. She's fantastic! What are your interests?

Please write and send a photo.
Clara Ferreira

6 Copy the chart in your notebook.

Days:	Monday, ...
Months:	October, ...
Names of places:	Chicago, ...
Nationalities and languages:	English, ...

7 Rewrite the words with capital letters. Complete the chart in exercise 6.

wednesday bogotá may argentina
brazilian thursday toronto august
spanish friday june tuesday
south america portuguese february

8 Check your reply to Clara. Are the capital letters correct?

Pronunciation

Counting syllables

9 🎧 Listen and count the number of syllables. Then listen and repeat.

1 syllable	2 syllables	3 syllables
school	music	negative

10 🎧 Listen and count the number of syllables. Write the words in the chart in your notebook.

1 friend   4 important
2 favorite   5 science
3 aren't   6 Spanish

⬤ **Finished?**

Look at exercise 6. Think of five more English words with one, two, or three syllables.
yes (1); hello (2); exercise (3)

Progress Check 1

School subjects

1 Write the subjects.

Interests

2 Match the words in the box with pictures 1–6.

1   karate

> photography   music   aerobics
> computers   ~~karate~~   chess

be: affirmative and negative

3 Write the correct verb forms.

> Ana and I (**1**) **are** / **we're** friends. We (**2**) **'s** / **'re** in the same class at school. Ana (**3**) **she is** / **is** interested in music. I prefer art. (**4**) **I'm** / **I are** in a photography club. The teachers in the club (**5**) **is** / **are** great, but I'm not an expert and my photos (**6**) **isn't** / **aren't** very good!

be: questions

4 Complete the speech bubbles.

Subject pronouns and interrogative pronouns

5 Choose the correct words.

> **Where** / **Who** is the book?
>
> **It's** / **She's** here.

1 **Who** / **When** are they?

We're / **They're** Jessica and Rachel.

2 **When** / **Where** are Nick and Scott?

They're / **You're** at school.

3 **What** / **Who** is her name?

She's / **Her** name is Clara.

4 **When** / **What time** are the exams?

They're / **It's** next week.

2 ○ Movie magic

Take a look!

Find the pages where you:
- read about a special effects artist.
- speak about your possessions.
- listen to two teenagers talking about their movie collection.

Vocabulary

Parts of the face

1 Match the words in the box with the photos.

> eyes   nose   mouth   ears   long hair
> short hair   dark hair   blonde hair   skin
> beard   moustache   teeth

2 🎧 Listen and repeat the words in exercise 1.

● VOCABULARY • PAGE 125

① Johnny Depp

② Scarlett Johansson

Reading

1 🎧 Read and listen.

Three faces, one model

Interview with Lars Carlsson, a special effects artist

Lars, what's your job?
I'm a special effects artist. I create faces for the movies, TV, and the theater.

You have a great job.
Yes, it's very interesting. The faces are all different.

The photos are good. Those red eyes are fantastic!
Thank you. I have a very good model. Her name's Karolina. She's my friend.

Who is the model in the other photos?
It's Karolina in all three photos!

Wow! Describe the real Karolina.
Karolina has long blonde hair. She has green eyes and fair skin. She doesn't have a moustache!

Ha, ha! What's your favorite face?
I don't have a favorite, but Karolina's favorite face has a long nose and black hair.

Lars, thank you very much.
Thank you.

2 **Read the interview again. Are the sentences true or false?**

Lars is an actor. *False.*

1 Lars has an interesting job.
2 The model is very good.
3 Lars is Karolina's boyfriend.
4 Lars's favorite face is picture 2.
5 Karolina's favorite face is picture 3.

> **Look!**
>
> **Possessive 's**
> Lars Carlsson's friend is the model.
> Karolina's favorite face has a long nose and black hair.

(● GRAMMAR • PAGE 116)

Pronunciation

Word stress (1)

Two-syllable words are stressed on their first or second syllable.

3 🎧 **Listen and repeat. Copy the chart in your notebook.**

First syllable	Second syllable
monster	cor**rect**

Monster!

Correct.

4 🎧 **Listen and write the words in the chart. Then listen and repeat.**

1 model	**3** describe
2 create	**4** special

Exploring grammar

have: affirmative and negative

5 **Look at the text in exercise 1. Then complete the chart with the correct form of *have*.**

Affirmative

I / You / We / They	have	a great job.
He / She / It	(1)	green eyes.

Negative

I / You / We / They	(2)	a favorite.
He / She / It	(3)	a moustache.

⬤ **GRAMMAR · PAGE 116**

6 **Complete the sentences. Use affirmative and negative forms of *have*.**

I *don't have* a beard.

1 We ...... classes on Friday.
2 We ...... an exam on Friday.
3 My English teacher ...... blonde hair.
4 My English teacher ...... dark hair.
5 I ...... blue eyes.
6 I ...... brown eyes.

7 **Look at photos 1–3 on page 14. Complete the descriptions of Karolina. Use the words in the chart.**

Verbs	Nouns		
has	nose	eyes	mouth
doesn't have	hair	skin	nose

1 In this photo she has white ...... and a very long .... Her ...... is very red.
2 She ...... long hair now. She has short ...... and a moustache.
3 Here she ...... red hair and red .... Her ...... is big.

Speaking

8 **Work in pairs. Describe a person in the class to your partner.**

A: She has long dark hair. She has fair skin and a small nose. Who is she?

B: It's Gisela.

⬤ **Finished?**

Write a description of your favorite actor or actress.

My favorite actress is Keira Knightley. She has ...

Vocabulary

Possessions

1   **Look at Cathy and Nick's movie collection. Match the words in the box with objects 1–7 in the photo. Which objects are not in the photo?**

> CD   book   DVD   computer game
> photo   comic   action figure   poster
> watch   mug

🔵 **VOCABULARY · PAGE 125**

2   🎧 **Listen and repeat the objects in exercise 1.**

Listening

3   🎧 **Before you listen, guess the answers to the questions. Then listen and check.**

1   How many posters do they have?

    a   8   **b**   18

2   How many comics do they have?

    a   21   **b**   71

3   How many action figures do they have?

    a   37   **b**   87

4   Does Cathy have the autograph of a famous person?

    a   Yes, she does.   **b**   No, she doesn't.

5   Do they have a website?

    a   Yes, they do.   **b**   No, they don't.

Exploring grammar

have: questions

4 **Look at exercise 3. Then copy and complete the chart with *do*, *does*, *don't*, *doesn't*, and *have*.**

Questions

Do I / we / you / they (1) ...... he / she / it		(2) ...... a website?
How many posters (3) ...... you have ? How many photos (4) ...... she (5) ...... ?		

Short answers

Yes,	I / we / you / they	do.
	he / she / it	does.
No,	I / we / you / they	don't.
	he / she / it	doesn't.

⬤ GRAMMAR · PAGE 116

5 **Complete the questions. Then write true answers.**

How many classes *do* we *have* today?
Seven.

1 How many English books ...... you ...... ?

2 ...... this book ...... 112 pages?

3 ...... your teacher ...... brown eyes?

4 ...... Cathy and Nick ...... red hair ?

5 How many DVDs ...... they ...... ?

6 **Put the words in order.**

How many / have? / CDs / you / do
How many CDs do you have?

1 does / pages / this book / How many / have?

2 you / have / a computer? / Do

3 DVDs / have? / do / How many / you

4 Do / have / you / a favorite movie?

5 you / a brother? / Do / have

7 🎧 **Listen and check your answers. Then listen and repeat.**

Speaking

8 **Work in pairs. Ask and answer the questions in exercise 6.**

A: *How many CDs do you have?*
B: *Twelve.*

9 **Think of more questions. Work in pairs. Ask and answer the questions.**

A: *Do you have a TV?*
B: *Yes, I do.*
A: *How many TVs do you have?*
B: *We have two.*

⬤ **Finished?**

Write about your things. Then tell your partner.
I have three posters in my room.
I don't have a computer.

Listening

1 🎧 Mel and Rob are talking about Mel's week. Listen and complete the information.

Mel's week

Movie shoot:	Wednesday and (1) ......
Meeting:	Sunday
TV interview:	(2) ......
Classes:	Monday, Tuesday, and (3) ......
Party:	(4) ......

Mel White – Schoolgirl star

movie shoot
classes

TV interview

party

Speaking

2 Imagine that you are a movie star. Write your day planner for next week. Use four activities in the box.

TV interview   party   movie shoot
exam   meeting   classes

Monday:

Tuesday:

Wednesday:

Thursday:

Friday:

Saturday:

Sunday:

Look!

Prepositions of time

on Monday	**on** February 18th
in February	**in** 2001
at three o'clock	**at** half past ten

🔵 GRAMMAR • PAGE 116

3 Work in pairs. Ask and answer questions about your day planner.

A: *Do you have classes next week?*

B: *No, I don't.*

A: *Do you have a TV interview?*

B: *Yes, I do. It's on Tuesday.*

Writing

A personal description: using notes

4 Read the description of Orlando Bloom and complete the notes.

Orlando Bloom is a British movie star. He's 1m80 tall and he has dark hair and brown eyes. Orlando's interested in soccer and likes Manchester United. He has one sister called Samantha. Some of his famous movies are *Troy* and *The Lord of the Rings* and *Pirates of the Caribbean*.

Screen magazine – Star profile

Name	Orlando Bloom
Nationality	British
Occupation	(1) ......
Height	(2) ......
Hair	(3) ......
Eyes	(4) ......
Interests	(5) ......
Brothers / sisters	(6) ......
Famous films	(7) ......

5 Write a description of Cameron Diaz. Use the information in the notes.

Cameron Diaz is an American actress. She's ...

Screen magazine – Star profile

Name	Cameron Diaz
Nationality	American
Occupation	actress and model
Height	1m75
Hair	blonde
Eyes	blue
Interests	cats
Brothers / sisters	one sister, Chimene
Famous films	*Charlie's Angels, Shrek, Vanilla Sky*

● Finished?

Imagine you are a famous movie star. Write sentences about your life.

On Monday, I have a meeting with Universal Studios.

Progress Check 2

Parts of the face

1 Match the words in the box with the parts of the face 1–8.

1 eyes

> short hair   fair skin   ~~eyes~~   beard
> moustache   nose   mouth   ear

WANTED!
$10,000

1
2
3
4
5
6
7
8

CRAZY CARL ROBERTS

Possessions

2 Name the objects in photos 1–6.

1 action figure

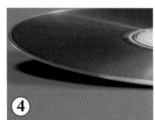

have: affirmative and negative

3 Look at the picture. Write sentences with affirmative and negative forms of *have*.

> They / a cat.
> They *don't have* a cat.

1 He / a watch.
2 She / a dog.
3 He / a dog.
4 He / a comic.
5 They / a camera.
6 They / pens.

have: questions

4 Put the words in the correct order. Then look at the picture and answer the questions.

> they / cat? / Do / have / a
> *Do they have a cat?*
> *No, they don't.*

1 he / dog? Does / a / have
2 Does / camera? / she / have / a
3 have / she / Does / a / dog?
4 they / Have / pens? / do
5 he / Does / have / watch? / a
6 have / Does / she / glasses?

The World of English 1

Brook Park
(pages 22 and 23)

Revision: *be* and *have*

Function: Greetings and introductions

1 Where's Viki from?

Culture File
(pages 24 and 25)

Topic: **Families**

2 Who is in the photo?

The World of Pop
(page 26)

Artist: **Britney Spears**
Country: **U.S.**

Song: **Lucky**

3 What are Britney's hobbies?

Brook Park

Nice to meet you

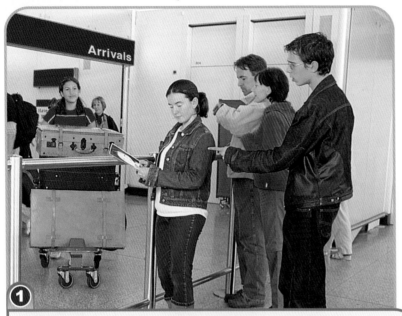

1

Mr. Daley	Well, where is she? Why's she late? What's her name?
Mrs. Daley	Her name's Victoria.
Paul	Is she a Cubs fan? Or is she a White Sox fan?
Sally	She's an exchange student from Colombia, Paul. She probably likes a Colombian baseball team. Look, here's her photo.
Paul	Oh wow. She's cute. Is that her?

2

Mrs. Daley	Uh, excuse me. Are you Victoria?
Viki	Yes, that's right.
Mrs. Daley	Hello, Victoria. Nice to meet you. I'm Pam Daley.
Viki	Oh, hello. Nice to meet you. Please call me Viki.
Mrs. Daley	Oh, OK. Viki, this is my daughter, Sally.
Sally	Hi, Viki.

3

Paul	Viki! What do you have in here?
Mr. Daley	Oh, no! My golf things are still in the car.
Paul	We don't have space for all this, Dad.
Mr. Daley	No, you're right, Paul. Listen, do me a favor.
Paul	What, go on the bus? With those? Oh, Dad!

4

Paul	Wait a minute! I only have one dollar.

5 Later ...

Sally	Oh, hi, Paul. Good game of golf?
Paul	Ha, ha, very funny. Hi, Viki! Welcome to Chicago. Welcome to the crazy Daley family!

Reading

1 🎧 **Read and listen to Brook Park episode 1 again. Then answer the questions.**

1 What are the names of the people in the story?

2 Who is Viki?

3 What does Mr. Daley have in his car?

4 How much money does Paul have?

Useful expressions

2 **Find the expressions in the story and check their meaning.**

1 Excuse me.

2 Nice to meet you.

3 Do me a favor.

4 Wait a minute!

Dialog

Greetings and introductions

3 🎧 **Look at this extract from Brook Park episode 1. Listen and repeat. Concentrate on your rhythm and intonation.**

A: Uh, excuse me. Are you Victoria?

B: Yes, that's right.

A: Hello, Victoria. Nice to meet you. I'm Pam Daley.

B: Oh, hello. Nice to meet you. Please call me Viki.

A: Oh, OK. Viki, this is my daughter, Sally.

C: Hi, Viki.

4 **Think of people who you want to meet. Write a list.**

1 a pop star   3 a sports star

2 a movie star   4 a model

5 **In groups of three, discuss your ideas from exercise 4. Use the dialog in exercise 3 as a model. Substitute the blue words to make your own dialogs.**

A: Uh, excuse me. Are you Ricky Martin?

B: Yes, that's right.

A: Hello, Mr. Martin. Nice to meet you. I'm Gabriela.

B: Oh, hello. Nice to meet you. Please call me Ricky.

A: Oh, OK. Ricky, this is my friend, Valeria.

C: Hi, Ricky.

Culture File 1

Families

1 Work in pairs. Discuss the questions.

1 Who are the families in these photos?

2 What are the names of the people?

3 How are they related?

My name's Sally Daley. I'm thirteen years old and I'm from the United States. I live in Chicago, a big city in the Midwest in the state of Illinois. I live with my parents and my brother. My parents' names are Pam and Mike, and my brother's name is Paul. He's fourteen.

I have grandparents, an uncle, an aunt, and a cousin here in Chicago. We see them a lot. Grandma and Grandpa Daley are my dad's parents. They have a nice apartment.

My Uncle Patrick is their son – he's my dad's brother. He's married to Aunt Jane and they have a daughter, my cousin Marina. Marina's fourteen and we're good friends.

Our other relatives live in Florida. We only see them during the summer vacation. My mom's parents live near Miami, and her sister lives in Orlando. Aunt Lynn isn't married, but she has a boyfriend.

My father has a computer store in downtown Chicago. He's a computer expert. We have an awesome computer at home, and we have a family website! My mom is an English teacher at my school. In fact, she's my English teacher!

We have a nice house and a big yard. We have two pets – a cat called Cleo and a dog called Maxie. I have lots of friends, and I have a pen pal in the U.K. His name's Ricky.

2 Read the text and describe the people's relationship to Sally.

Paul	*Sally's brother*
Patrick	(1) ......
Pam	(2) ......
Grandma Daley	(3) ......
Marina	(4) ......
Mike	(5) ......
Jane	(6) ......

3 Read the text again and answer the questions.

Where is Chicago?

It's in the United States. It's in Illinois in the Midwest.

1 How old is Paul?

2 Is Uncle Patrick married?

3 Who is in Miami?

4 What is Mr. Daley's job?

5 What is special about Sally's English teacher?

6 What pets does Sally have?

7 Who is Sally's pen pal?

4 Ricky is Sally's pen pal.
Look at his family tree.
Complete 1–7 with each
person's relationship
to Ricky.

Ben
grandfather

Jenna
(1) ......

Leon
(2) ......

Karen
(3) ......

Emily
(4) ......

Jim
(5) ......

Ricky
Me!

Helen
(6) ......

Tom
(7) ......

5 🎧 **Listen to Ricky and choose the correct answers.**

Ricky is ...

a (thirteen.)　　**b** sixteen.

1 Ricky's parents are ...

a divorced.　　**b** married.

2 Ricky lives with ...

a his mother.　　**b** his mother and his sister.

3 Ricky's grandparents live in ...

a Cambridge.　　**b** Manchester.

4 Ricky's family have ...

a a cat.　　**b** a dog.

5 Ricky's father lives in ...

a a house.　　**b** an apartment.

6 Ricky's mother is ...

a an actor.　　**b** a writer.

7 Ricky's Aunt Emily is ...

a a housewife.　　**b** a doctor.

6 **What do Sally and Ricky have in common? Are the sentences true or false?**

1 They are thirteen.

2 They have a brother.

3 They have one cousin.

4 They have a dog.

Project

Draw your family tree. Include:

- the names of the people
- their relationship to you
- their jobs
- their pets

Add pictures to your family tree.

The World of Pop 1

Britney Spears

Full name: Britney Jean Spears

Date of birth: December 2nd, 1981

Place of birth: Kentwood, Louisiana, U.S.

Height: 1m63

Brothers and sisters: Bryan, Jamie Lynn

Children: Sean Preston, Jayden James

Britney Spears (U.S.)

1 **Look at the information about Britney Spears. Answer the questions.**

1 What is Britney's middle name?

2 How old is she now?

3 How many brothers and sisters does she have?

4 Describe Britney's face.

2 **Complete the song with the words in the box.**

> world   dream   girl   door   morning
> makeup   tears   star   heart   girl

3 🎧 **Listen to the song and check your answers.**

Lucky

1 Early *morning*, she wakes up.
2 Knock, knock, knock on the (**1**) ......
3 It's time for (**2**) ......, perfect smile,
4 It's you they're all waiting for.
5 They go:
6 "Isn't she lovely, this Hollywood (**3**) ......?"
7 And they say:

(Chorus)
8 She's so lucky, she's a (**4**) ......,
9 But she cry, cry, cries in her lonely (**5**) ......, thinking
10 "If there's nothing missing in my life,
11 Then why do these (**6**) ...... come at night?"

12 Lost in an image, in a (**7**) ......
13 But there's no one there to wake her up
14 And the (**8**) ...... is spinning
15 And she keeps on winning
16 But tell me what happens when it stops?
17 They go:
18 "Isn't she lovely, this Hollywood (**9**)......?"
19 And they say:

(Repeat chorus)

Glossary

15 keeps on = continues

4 **Are the sentences true or false?**

1 Lucky is a Hollywood star.

2 She is very happy.

3 She is lonely.

4 She is popular.

3 Body and mind

Take a look!

Find the pages where you:
- complete a questionnaire about your lifestyle.
- listen to a brain expert.
- talk about your likes and dislikes.

Vocabulary

Food and drink

1 Match photos 1–10 with the words in the box. Then listen and repeat.

> fish   meat   vegetables   juice   bread
> fruit   cereal   coffee   desserts   snacks

2 Complete the chart with foods and drinks.

Good for you	Bad for you
juice	

● VOCABULARY • PAGE 126

Reading

1 🎧 **Read and listen. Then match names 1–5 with photos a–e.**

1	Mary	4	Ellie
2	Nick	5	Mike and Rita
3	Wayne and Stacey		

2 Read the texts again and answer the questions.

1 Who is a vegetarian?
2 Who is a chocoholic?
3 Does Nick have a healthy diet? Why?
4 What are Wayne and Stacey's favorite drinks?
5 What is Ellie's favorite food?

Mary and Nick

Hi. My name's Mary and this is my brother, Nick. I don't eat meat. I prefer vegetables and salads. I like cereal in the morning, but my favorite food is chocolate. I'm a real chocoholic! When I'm with my parents in a restaurant, I have a big chocolate dessert. My brother, Nick, eats burgers and snacks non-stop. His diet is terrible! He doesn't like vegetables, and he doesn't eat fruit.

Wayne and Stacey

We're P.E. teachers and our diet is very healthy. We eat a lot of pasta, vegetables, and fruit. We aren't vegetarians: we like meat but we prefer fish. We don't drink coffee. We prefer juice or water.

The Brown family: Rita, Mike, and Ellie

Rita and Mike like Chinese and Indian food. They eat a lot of curry and rice. They don't eat snacks or desserts. Ellie doesn't like curry. Her favorite food is pizza. She doesn't like burgers, and she doesn't eat a lot of vegetables.

Look!

Possessive adjectives

My favorite food is chocolate.
His diet is terrible!

⬤ GRAMMAR · PAGE 117

Exploring grammar

Simple present: affirmative and negative

3 Complete the table with *I*, *we*, and *she*.

Affirmative and negative		
(1) ...... You (2) ...... They	eat don't eat	meat.
He (3) ...... It	eats doesn't eat	meat.

⬤ **GRAMMAR • PAGE 117**

4 **Choose the correct form of the verb.**

Healthy people **don't eat** / **eat** vegetables.

1 Nick **eats** / **doesn't eat** vegetables.
2 My friends **drink** / **don't drink** coffee.
3 Wayne **drinks** / **doesn't drink** juice.
4 Vegetarians **eat** / **don't eat** meat or fish.
5 Rita **likes** / **doesn't like** curry.

5 **Complete the text with the correct verb forms.**

The International

David and Tessa's parents have a restaurant: "The International". David and Tessa *like* (like) international food and they (**1**) ...... (eat) in the restaurant every Saturday.

David (**2**) ...... (not eat) meat. He (**3**) ...... (prefer) vegetables. He (**4**) ...... (not eat) salad, but he (**5**) ...... (like) rice. His favorite food is fruit.

Tessa (**6**) ...... (not eat) curry or rice. She (**7**) ...... (eat) meat and she (**8**) ...... (like) Brazilian and Italian food. Her favorite food is soup.

Speaking

6 **Work in pairs. Look at The International Restaurant menu. Tell your partner about the food you like and don't like.**

I don't like salad. I like soup.

I don't like Chinese food. I prefer Italian food.

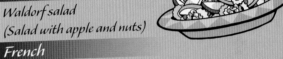

The International Restaurant

Appetizers

American
Waldorf salad
(Salad with apple and nuts)

French
French Onion Soup
Salad Niçoise (salad with tuna, beans, egg, potatoes, tomatoes and anchovies)

Main Courses

Indian
Vegetable curry and Indian naan bread

Brazilian
Feijoada (pork with black beans)

Chinese
Chicken chop suey and rice

Italian
Spaghetti Bolognese (pasta, meat, and tomatoes)

Pronunciation

Third person -s: /ɪz/, /s/, and /z/

7 🎧 **Listen and repeat. Which verb ends with the sound /ɪz/?**

1 walks   2 swims   3 bikes   4 watches

8 🎧 **Listen and repeat. Which verbs end with the sound /ɪz/?**

1 plays   2 exercises   3 likes   4 sleeps
5 eats   6 drinks   7 relaxes   8 cries

⬤ **Finished?**

Write a menu for your favorite restaurant.

Vocabulary

Activities

1 Find the verbs in the questionnaire. Check their meanings.

> walk   watch TV   sleep   bike   swim
> play computer games   relax   exercise

2 Listen and repeat the words in exercise 1.

(VOCABULARY · PAGE 126)

Speaking

3 Work in pairs. Complete the questionnaire and check your answers. How healthy are you?

Listening

4 Mary and her grandfather are completing the questionnaire. Read the questions and guess the grandfather's answers.

1 Does he walk two kilometers every day?
2 Does he watch TV every day?
3 Does he sleep for nine hours a night?
4 Does he play computer games?
5 Does he bike or swim?

5 Listen and check your answers.

Lifestyle questionnaire

1

Do you walk two kilometers every day?

a Yes, I do.
b No, I don't.
c It depends.

2

Do you watch TV every day?

a No, I don't.
b Yes, I watch TV for one or two hours a day.
c Yes, I watch TV for three or four hours a day.

3

Do you sleep for nine hours a night?

a No, I don't.
b It depends.
c Yes, I do.

4

Do you play computer games?

a No, I don't. I prefer to relax in other ways.
b Yes, I play for one or two hours a week.
c Yes, I play for three or four hours a week.

5

Do you bike or swim?

a I bike and swim.
b I bike but I don't swim.
c I swim but I don't bike.
d I don't bike or swim. I don't exercise.

0–3
Oh no! You don't have very healthy habits.

4–6
Mmmmmm. Not bad. What are your healthy and unhealthy habits?

7–10
Wow! You're healthy. Congratulations.

1 a2 b0 c1
2 a2 b1 c0
3 a0 b1 c2
4 a2 b1 c0
5 a2 b1 c1 d0

Exploring grammar

Simple present: questions and short answers

6 Look at the questionnaire and exercise 4. Complete the chart with *do, does*, and *don't*.

Questions		
Do	I / you / we / they	sleep?
(1)	he / she / it	
Short answers		
Yes, No,	I / you / we / they	(2) .... (3) ....
Yes, No,	he / she / it	does. doesn't.

⬤ GRAMMAR • PAGE 117

7 Put the words in the correct order. Then write short answers.

Do you read comics?

Yes, I do.

you / watch TV? / Do

Do you watch TV?
Yes, I do.

1 Does / play computer games? / your father /

2 you / Do / exercise?

3 listen to music? / Does / your mother /

4 Do / sleep / in class? / you /

5 Does / walk to school? / your teacher /

6 eat vegetables? / you / Do

8 Complete the questions with *Do* or *Does*.

Do you relax after school?

1 ...... your father bike to work?

2 ...... you watch a lot of DVDs?

3 ...... your mother eat meat?

4 ...... you go to the dentist?

5 ...... you walk to school?

6 ...... your teacher drink coffee?

Speaking

9 In pairs, ask and answer questions in exercise 8.

A: Do you relax after school?

B: Yes, I do. I watch TV and listen to music.

Simple present: spelling rules

10 Look at the examples.

sleep ➤ sleep**s**
watch ➤ watch**es**
go ➤ go**es**

⬤ GRAMMAR • PAGE 117

11 Write the third person singular form of the verbs.

1 relax   **2** walk   **3** like   **4** do

Finished?

If you watch TV for one hour a day, your total for one year is 365 hours, and in ten years it's 3,650 hours! What are your ten year totals for ...

1 sleep?   **3** computer games?

2 TV?   **4** English classes?

Listening

1 Are the sentences true or false?
Guess the answers.

1 The human brain weighs five kilos.

2 Elephants have big brains.

3 Different parts of the brain control different actions.

4 Your brain is active when you sleep.

5 Exercise is good for your brain.

2 Listen to the interview and check your answers to exercise 1.

USPR Science special

BODY AND MIND

Interview with brain expert Doctor John Nicholls.

Speaking

3 Work pairs. Ask and answer the questions in the brain test. Write your partner's answers. Then check the key.

A: *Do you like math?*
B: *No, I don't.*

The *Brain* test

Are you a future pop star or doctor? The answer is in your brain.

① Do you like math?
Yes, I do. (L)   No, I don't. (R)

② Do you like science?
Yes, I do. (L)   No, I don't. (R)

③ Do you prefer art (R) or ICT (L)?

④ Do you like reading and writing?
Yes, I do. (R) No, I don't. (L)

⑤ Do you listen to music?
Yes, I do. (R) No, I don't. (L)

⑥ Do you play a musical instrument?
Yes, I do. (R)   No, I don't. (L)

⑦ Do you like chess?
Yes, I do. (L) No, I don't. (R)

⑧ Do you play computer games?
Yes, I do. (L)   No, I don't. (R)

The brain test

(L) answers	(R) answers
0 – 3	5 – 8

You are artistic, imaginative, creative, and musical.

| 4 | 4 |

You are logical and creative. Interesting combination!

| 5 – 8 | 0 – 3 |

You are logical, mathematical, and scientific.

Writing

Lifestyles: *and* and *but*

4 Look at the chart about Hannah and James. Complete the sentences with *and* or *but*.

	Hannah	James
listen to music	✓	✓
play an instrument	✗	✓
play chess	✓	✗
play computer games	✓	✗
math	✗	✓
art	✓	✗

Hannah listens to music, but she doesn't play an instrument.

1 James listens to music ...... he plays an instrument.

2 Hannah plays chess ...... computer games.

3 James likes math ...... he doesn't like art.

4 Hannah doesn't like math ...... she likes art.

5 Join the sentences. Use *and* and *but*.

I read books. I like magazines.

I read books, and I like magazines.

1 I eat pasta. I don't eat rice.

2 I like music. I don't listen to heavy metal.

3 I like math. I like science. I don't like P.E.

4 I play chess. I prefer sports.

6 Write about a friend's lifestyle. Use *and* and *but*. Include information about:

- school
- reading
- food and drink
- music
- games

Study skills

Remembering vocabulary

Try to remember vocabulary in different ways:

a with pictures.

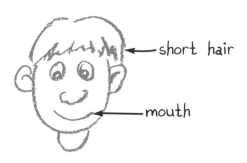

b with diagrams.

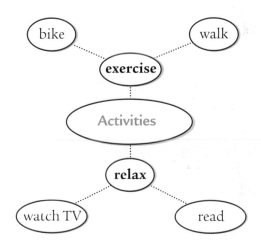

7 What other methods do you use for remembering vocabulary?

8 Choose a method of remembering vocabulary for these word groups.

1 food and drink

2 school subjects

3 possessions

4 families

Finished?

Add more words to the diagram for Activities.

Progress Check 3

Food and drink

1 **Put the letters in order.**

shif – *fish*	**3** acskns	**6** tame
1 daber	**4** uicej	**7** uitfr
2 cralee	**5** fefeoc	**8** getvelseba

Activities

2 **Match expressions 1–6 with pictures a–f.**

1d

1 swim	**4** sleep
2 bike	**5** play computer games
3 walk	**6** watch TV

Simple present: affirmative and negative

3 **Choose the correct form of the verbs.**

In my free time I **read** / **don't read** a lot. I like books, but I (1) **like** / **don't like** comics. I'm interested in music, and I (2) **listen** / **don't listen** to CDs in my room. Guitar music is my favorite, but I (3) **play** / **don't play** an instrument. Oh, and I (4) **eat** / **don't eat** a lot of chocolate!

Simple present: spelling rules

4 **Write the simple present third person singular form of the verbs.**

listen – *listens*

1 exercise	**4** relax
2 watch	**5** go
3 play	**6** bike

Simple present: questions and short answers

5 **Look at the picture of Laura and Bill. Complete the questions with *Do* or *Does*. Then write short answers.**

Does Bill like photography?
Yes, he does.

1 ...... the dog like their food?

2 ...... Laura speak Italian?

3 ...... Laura and Bill like Italian food?

4 ...... the waiter play an instrument?

5 ...... Bill like the music?

4 Total sports

Take a look!

Find the pages where you:
- read about an American football player.
- read about some American teenagers.
- write about your perfect sports day.

Vocabulary

Sports

1 🎧 Match the words in the box with photos 1–9. Then listen and repeat.

> tennis   biking   soccer   field hockey
> swimming   skiing   table tennis
> basketball   volleyball

2 🎧 Listen to the sounds. Write the sports that you hear.

3 What sports do you like?

⬤ VOCABULARY • PAGE 126

Reading

1 🎧 Read and listen. Match the names of the people with photos 1–4.

My name's **Peter** and these are my friends. We're all crazy about sports. My favorite sports are basketball and soccer. I'm a Miami Heat fan, and I always watch them on TV.

Louise never plays soccer. She prefers basketball. We're on a mixed team at school, and we usually play with the team on weekends. She's very good.

Lauren isn't on the basketball team. Her sport is tennis. I sometimes watch her. I think that she's a future champion. She teaches me, but I'm not very good. She always beats me.

Patrick is in a biking club. He has a great bike, and he often bikes 60 or 70 kilometers on Saturdays. I like biking, but I never go with him.

2 **Read the text again and answer the questions.**

1 Which team does Peter watch?
2 Does Louise play soccer?
3 When does Louise play basketball?
4 What sport does Patrick like?
5 Does Peter like biking?
6 Is Lauren good at tennis?
7 When does Patrick go biking?
8 Who does Lauren teach?
9 Is Louise on a girls' basketball team?

Exploring grammar
Adverbs of frequency

3 Look at the texts on page 36 and complete the sentences with the adverbs of frequency.

0% She ...... plays soccer.

I ...... watch her.

He ...... bikes 60 or 70 kilometers.

We ...... play on weekends.

100% I ...... watch them on TV.

4 Choose the correct word to complete the rule.

Adverbs of frequency come **before** / **after** the verb.

GRAMMAR · PAGE 118

5 Look at the chart. Write sentences with adverbs of frequency.

Saturday sports

	⚽	🎾	🏀
Peter	****	**	****
Patrick	o	*	**
Louise	o	**	***
Lauren	*	****	o

Key: ° never * sometimes ** often *** usually **** always

Peter / soccer

Peter always plays soccer on Saturdays.

1 Patrick and Louise / soccer

2 Lauren / tennis

3 Patrick / tennis

4 Louise / basketball

5 Peter and Louise / tennis

6 Lauren / basketball

6 Complete the sentences with adverbs of frequency.

I *sometimes* play table tennis.

1 I go to soccer games.

2 I buy a sports magazine or newspaper.

3 My friends play on a sports team.

4 My father watches sports on TV.

5 I bike ten kilometers.

Speaking

7 Work in pairs. Ask and answer questions about sports. Use the ideas in exercise 6.

A: Do you play table tennis?
B: Yes, sometimes.

Subject and object pronouns

8 Complete the chart with *them*, *him*, *us*, and *her*.

Subject pronouns	Object pronouns
I	me
you	you
he	(1) ......
she	(2) ......
it	it
we	(3) ......
they	(4) ......

GRAMMAR · PAGE 118

9 Complete the sentences with object pronouns.

He's not very good at tennis. I always beat *him*.

1 I'm great. You never beat ....

2 We're in her P.E. class. She teaches ....

3 I don't like sports magazines. I don't read ....

4 She plays tennis and I always watch ....

5 Rafael Nadal is good at tennis. I like ....

Finished?

Write about your family and friends. What sports do they like?

Vocabulary

Daily routines

1 🎧 **Read and listen. Find the third person *-s* form of the verbs.**

travel – *travels*

1	have dinner	**5**	have breakfast
2	go to bed	**6**	practice
3	get up	**7**	get changed
4	take a shower	**8**	have lunch

2 **Guess the meaning of the verbs. Then check in a dictionary.**

◯ **VOCABULARY • PAGE 126**

The Keith Alexander fan club

The American football star prepares for the big game

Friday

16:00 Keith and the team go to the airport in Miami. Saturday's game is in Los Angeles, 4,000 kilometers away. Keith often travels 5,000 kilometers in a week.

20:00 Keith has dinner with the team in a restaurant. They eat a lot of healthy "energy" food: pasta, potatoes, meat, and fish. Keith is 1m98 and he weighs 143 kilos. He eats a lot!

21:30 Keith relaxes in the hotel. He usually reads or watches TV.

23:00 He goes to bed.

Saturday

7:00 Keith gets up and he takes a shower.

7:30 He has breakfast.

9:00 Practice. Keith has six practices every week. In total he practices for 24 hours a week.

12:30 Keith takes another shower and gets changed. Then he has lunch with the team.

16:00 The team prepares for the game. The players get changed. Their protective equipment is very important. It weighs twelve kilos.

17:00 The big game. 78,000 fans are at the game, and millions of people watch it on TV. Keith is an important player. He knows it and the fans know it. This is the moment of truth.

Reading

3 **Read the text again and answer the questions from Keith's fans.**

1 How many kilometers does Keith travel in a week?

2 Where does he have dinner?

3 Who does he have dinner with?

4 What does Keith eat?

5 How does he relax?

6 What time does Keith go to bed the night before a game?

7 How often does Keith practice?

8 When do the players get changed?

9 How many people go to the game?

Exploring grammar

Simple present: interrogative pronouns

4 **Look at the questions in exercise 3. Underline the interrogative pronouns.**

How ...?	What ...?
How often ...?	What time ...?
How many ...?	Where ...?
	Who ...?
	When ...?

GRAMMAR · PAGE 118

5 **Put the words in order. Then answer the questions.**

live? / Where / you / do

Where do you live? I live in ...

1 What / watch / do / on TV? / you

2 go / do / you / Where / with your friends?

3 do / have breakfast in bed? / you / How often

4 What sports / do / like? / you

5 do / you / How / travel to school?

6 What time / go to bed? / do / you

7 do / sports / play? / How many / you

8 have / do / you / dinner with? / Who

6 **Write questions for the interview with Sergei Fetisov, a Russian ice hockey player.**

What's your name?

I'm Sergei Fetisov.

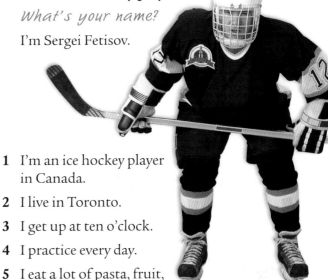

1 I'm an ice hockey player in Canada.

2 I live in Toronto.

3 I get up at ten o'clock.

4 I practice every day.

5 I eat a lot of pasta, fruit, and vegetables.

6 About 20,000 fans come every week.

7 I wear protective equipment including a helmet and pads.

7 🎧 **Listen and check. Then listen and repeat.**

Pronunciation

/h/

8 🎧 **Listen and repeat.**

1 how   2 who   3 he   4 has

9 🎧 **Listen and repeat.**

Harry has a healthy lunch with Helen.

Speaking

10 **Work in pairs. Choose a famous sportsperson you know. Ask and answer your questions from exercise 6.**

A: What's your name?
B: I'm ...

Finished?

Invent a sports star. Write about their routine.

Listening

1 **Look at the *No limits* brochure and answer the questions.**

> How many activities does *No limits* offer?
> *They offer three activities.*

1 What country is sand skiing from?

2 Which activity do you prefer?

3 What's the *No limits* telephone number?

No limits

The radical sports company
For more information, phone (604) 897–3824.

Summer activities.

Sand skiing
The new 50km/h sport from the U.S.

Kayaking
If you like excitement, this is for you!

Snowboarding
Our experts teach you the basics.

2 🎧 **Lauren is interested in the *No limits* activities. Listen and put a–c in order.**

a Lauren speaks to Kim, the receptionist at *No limits*.

b Lauren speaks to her mother.

c Lauren speaks to James.

3 🎧 **Listen again. Write the correct names.**

> Lauren   James   Kim

1 ...... is interested in sand skiing.

2 ...... thinks that the sand skiing is dangerous.

3 ...... doesn't like water.

4 ...... thinks that the snowboarding is expensive.

5 ...... recommends the kayaking.

4 🎧 **Complete the dialog with the words in the box. Then listen and check.**

> Goodbye   snowboarding   ~~speaking~~
> expensive   kayaking   courses

Kim: Hello, *No limits*. Kim *speaking*.

Lauren: Oh, hello. I'm calling about your **(1)** .... Can you tell me the price of the snowboarding?

Kim: Yes, the **(2)** ...... is $250.

Lauren: $250. Ooh! It's a bit **(3)** ....

Kim: Well, the **(4)** ...... is really good. That's only $100.

Lauren: $100. OK. Thanks very much. **(5)** ....

Kim: Goodbye. Thank you for calling.

Speaking

5 **Practice a new dialog.**

- Use the dialog in exercise 4.
- Change the people's names, the prices, and the names of the sports.
- Choose from these sports: bungee jumping, sailing, climbing, and hang-gliding.

Writing

first, next, after that, and *finally*

6 Read Lauren's competition entry and answer the questions.

No limits

Competition

Write about your perfect sports day, and win a free sports lesson!

My perfect sports day

First, I get up and I have breakfast in my hotel. I play tennis with Maria Sharapova, and then I take a shower. I have lunch with Fernando Alonso in an Italian restaurant.

Next, I watch Manchester United and Real Madrid play soccer.

After that, I have dinner with the teams, and I go to a disco with Ronaldo.

Finally, I go to my hotel and I go to bed.

1 What does Lauren do *first*?

2 What does she do *next*?

3 *After that*, what does she do?

4 *Finally*, what does she do?

7 Check the meaning of *first, next, after that*, and *finally*.

◯ VOCABULARY • PAGE 126

8 Make notes about your perfect sports day. Think about these things:

- What time do you get up?
- What do you do in the morning, afternoon, and evening?
- Where do you eat?
- Which sports stars do you meet?
- Where do you go?

9 Write about your perfect sports day. Use *first, next, after that*, and *finally*.

◯ Finished?

Make words from the letters on the scarf.
man, team

Progress Check 4

Sports

1 Write the names of the sports.

Daily routines

2 Complete the paragraph about Monica's day. Use the simple present of the verbs in the box.

get up   practice
have breakfast
go go go
have dinner
take a shower

Monica *gets up* at 8:00 and she (**1**) .... She (**2**) ...... at 8:30, and then she (**3**) ...... to school. At 4:00, she (**4**) ...... to soccer practice. She's on a team and she (**5**) ...... every Monday and Wednesday. After practice, she relaxes with her friends. She (**6**) ...... at 7:30 at home with her parents. After dinner, she reads or watches TV. She (**7**) ...... to bed at 10:00.

Adverbs of frequency

3 Look at the chart. Write sentences with *play* and adverbs of frequency.

Monica often plays tennis on Saturdays.

Saturday Sports	⚽	🎾
Monica	always	often
Tim	sometimes	often
Rachel	never	usually

1 Monica / soccer
2 Monica and Tim / tennis
3 Rachel / tennis
4 Tim / soccer
5 Rachel / soccer

Subject and object pronouns

4 Complete the sentences with the words in the box.

it us them her ~~him~~ me

He likes soccer, but I never play with *him*.

1 I like soccer. I watch ...... on TV.
2 I'm not very good at table tennis. Paul always beats ....
3 When Kevin and Sue go to the game I go with ....
4 Sarah is a good friend. I really like ....
5 Our teacher always gives ...... homework.

Simple present: interrogative pronouns

5 Complete the questions.

"*How often* do you watch TV?" "Every day."

1 "...... do you go to a soccer game?" "Every Saturday."
2 "...... do you have lunch?" "At one o'clock."
3 "...... do you get changed?" "After school."
4 "...... do you practice?" "At the sports center."
5 "...... people go to your school?" "About 1,000."

The World of English 2

Brook Park
(pages 44 and 45)

Review: simple present

Function: Buying things

1   What does Viki want to buy?

Culture File
(pages 46 and 47)

Topic: National sports

2   What are the national sports in the U.S., the U.K., and Canada?

The World of Pop
(page 48)

Artist: **Vanessa Amorosi**

Country: **Australia**

Song: **Absolutely Everybody**

3   Does Vanessa like animals?

Brook Park

Have some spirit!

1

Sally	Morning, Viki. How's the food? Dad makes a huge breakfast on Saturdays.
Viki	Oh, yes, it's good. I like it. It's … er … it's big.
Sally	Good. Listen, do you want to go to the mall later? I need to go to one or two stores.
Paul	She means one or two hundred stores.
Sally	Hey, don't be rude!

2

Viki	Excuse me. How much is this shirt?
Sales clerk	The shirts are all $29·95.
Viki	Oh, really? That's a little expensive.
Sally	Well, how about a scarf? They're $5.
Viki	OK. That's not bad.
Sally	It's a good deal! And red and white are the school colors.

3

Paul	Hey! It's a message from Dad – he's at the game with Mom. Let's go.
Viki	Oh, right, the baseball game. Is it at your high school?
Sally	Yes. We have great seats and our team is terrific.

4

Viki	What time does the game start?
Sally	In ten minutes. Your scarf is great!
Paul	Come on! Have some spirit! Here we go Brook Park. Here we go!
Viki	OK! Here we go Brook Park! Here we go!

Reading

1 🎧 **Read and listen to Brook Park episode 2 again. Then answer the questions.**

1 What does Viki think of the breakfast?

2 Where does Sally want to go?

3 Why doesn't Viki buy the shirt?

4 What does Viki buy?

5 What kind of game do Viki, Sally, and Paul go to?

Useful expressions

2 **Find the expressions in the story and check their meaning.**

1 Hey, don't be rude!

2 That's not bad.

3 It's a good deal!

4 Have some spirit!

Dialog

Shopping

3 🎧 **Look at this extract from Brook Park episode 2. Listen and repeat. Concentrate on your rhythm and intonation.**

A: Excuse me. How much is this shirt?

B: The shirts are all $29·95.

A: Oh, really? That's a little expensive.

C: Well, how about a scarf? They're $5.

A: OK. That's not bad.

B: It's a good deal!

4 **Look at the objects in the photo. Think of a price for each object.**

5 **In groups of three, discuss your ideas from exercise 4. Use the dialog in exercise 3 as a model. Substitute the blue words to make your own dialogs.**

A: Excuse me. How much are the scarves?

B: The scarves are all $20.

A: Oh, really? That's a little expensive.

C: Well, how about a calendar? They're $4·50.

A: OK. That's not bad.

Culture File 2

National sports

1 What is your national sport? Does your country have any famous sports people?

2 What do you know about baseball, soccer, and ice hockey? Write *B* for baseball, *S* for soccer, or *I* for ice hockey next to the words in the box.

> 11 players *S*   9 players   6 players
> goalkeeper   batter   World Series
> World Cup   league   New York Yankees
> Manchester United   goals   runs
> Toronto Maple Leafs

3 Read the text and answer the questions.

When is baseball season in the United States?
From April to October.

1 Where do the Red Sox play?
2 Name a city that has two teams.
3 How many leagues are in Major League Baseball?
4 What is the big competition in Major League Baseball?
5 Where is baseball popular outside of the United States? Name three other countries.
6 What percentage of baseball fans are women in the United States?

Baseball is the national sport of the United States. In the summer, all over the country, people watch and play baseball. The season is from April to October.

Major League Baseball (MLB) is everywhere in the United States. Most large cities have a team. For example, Boston has the Red Sox, and the Arizona Diamondbacks play in Phoenix. Very big cities have two teams. The Yankees and the Mets play in New York, and Chicago has the Cubs and the White Sox.

In Major League Baseball, there are two leagues, or groups of teams. They are the American League and the National League. At the end of the season, the winners of the two leagues play in the World Series. The World Series is the big competition. The winners are the world champions.

But, is the winner of the World Series really the world champion? People in Cuba, Panama, Venezuela, Mexico, Colombia, and Puerto Rico probably disagree! Baseball is also popular in these countries, and there are good baseball players there, too. Many of the players in the U.S. are from these countries. There are also good players from Japan, Korea, and Taiwan.

Major League Baseball has players from all over the world, but they are all men. So is baseball a man's sport? This is an interesting question. Almost 50% of U.S. baseball fans are women, and there are women's leagues in the United States and other countries. But the famous teams and famous players are all men ... at least, for now.

4 🎧 **Listen to an interview with sports writer, James Glenn. Number topics a–e in the order they are mentioned.**

a Canada's national sport.

b Countries where soccer is a national sport.

c The U.S. national sport.

d The National Hockey League.

e Soccer competitions.

5 🎧 **Listen to the interview again. Are the sentences true or false?**

Soccer is a national sport in the U.K.

True

1 The FA Premiership is for European soccer teams.

2 Only British teams compete in the Champions League.

3 Canada's national sport is ice hockey.

4 The ice hockey season is short.

5 All the players in the National Hockey League are Canadian.

6 There is a women's ice hockey league.

6 **Complete the table.**

Country	National Sport
1 U.S.	
2 Canada	
3 U.K.	

Project

Make a poster about your favorite team – a famous team or a school team, you choose! Give information about the following:

- the game
- the team members
- some recent results
- why you like them

Add pictures and photos to your poster.

The World of Pop 2

Vanessa Amorosi

Name: Vanessa Amorosi

Date of birth: August 8th, 1981

Place of birth: Melbourne, Australia

Brothers and sisters: Melissa, Natasha, Rebecca, Corey, and Anthony

Pets: horses, a bird, a frog, cats, dogs, a fish, a rat, and a camel

Interests: Vanessa has a farm. She is a vegetarian and she is interested in animal rights. She also works for childrens' charities.

First CD: *The Power*

Vanessa Amorosi (Australia)

1 Look at the information about Vanessa Amorosi. Answer the questions.

1 Where is Vanessa from?

2 When was Vanessa born?

3 Does Vanessa eat meat?

4 What color is Vanessa's hair?

2 Read the song. Choose the correct words.

3 🎧 **Listen to the song and check your answers.**

4 🎧 **Listen to the song again and look at a–f. According to the song what three things do we all need?**

a money	**d** a good friend
b a human touch	**e** a father
c food	**f** love

Absolutely Everybody

(Chorus)

1 Absolutely everybody,
2 Everybody, everybody.
3 Absolutely everybody
4 In the whole wide world.
5 Everybody breathes,
6 And everybody needs.
7 Absolutely everybody

8 Everybody needs a human (touch) / mouth.
9 I can't **(1) live / walk** without it,
10 It means too much to me.
11 Everybody needs one true **(2) pet / friend**,
12 Someone who'll be there 'til the very end.
13 And absolutely everybody **(3) breathes / reads**,
14 And everybody, everybody bleeds.
15 We're no different,
16 We're all the **(4) same / family**,
17 Players in the **(5) game / class**.
(Repeat chorus)

18 Absolutely everybody, *(repeat x4)*
19 Every boy and girl.
20 Every woman and **(6) child / person**,
21 Every father and **(7) teacher / son**,
22 I said now everyone,
23 Yes now everyone.

24 Everybody needs a human **(8) touch / arm**.
25 Everybody, everybody needs **(9) love / books**.
26 I'm no different,
27 I am just the same,
28 A player in the **(10) club / game**.

(Repeat chorus x2)

Glossary

12 the very end = the absolute end

22 said = past of "say"

27 just = exactly

5 Celebrations

Take a look!

Find the pages where you:

- listen to a conversation at a carnival.
- read about a celebration in Kenya.
- read about special days around the world.

Vocabulary

Celebrations

1 Look at photos 1–8 and write a list. Which celebrations are important for you?

Important for me	Not important for me
birthday	

🔴 **VOCABULARY • PAGE 127**

2 🎧 Listen and repeat celebrations 1–8.

3 When are the celebrations?

New Year's Day – January 1st

① New Year's Day

② birthday

③ Christmas

④ Easter

⑤ carnival

⑥ Halloween

⑦ Thanksgiving

⑧ Valentine's Day

Reading

1 🎧 **Read and listen. Match texts 1–6 with photos a–f.**

1
In this photo my brother James is reading a magazine. I'm speaking to him, but he isn't listening – typical!

2
It's December 31st and we're celebrating the New Year. It's called Hogmanay in Scotland. My brother is playing the bagpipes. They're a traditional Scottish instrument. They're very difficult to play. I prefer the guitar.

3
In this photo we're in class. Our teacher is speaking in Swahili, our language. Agriculture and English are my favorite school subjects.

4
We aren't studying now – we're dancing! We're all wearing traditional clothes. We're celebrating the harvest in our village. It's my favorite celebration.

5
Here we're making our costumes for carnival. I'm not wearing my costume right now. It's October now and carnival in Rio de Janeiro is in February or sometimes in March.

6
This is carnival in Rio. We don't have school today. People are playing music, singing, and dancing in the street. My parents aren't dancing. They're sitting in the crowd because they prefer to watch.

Carolina, Brazil

Paul, Scotland

Sesi and Sika, Kenya

2 **Read the text again and answer the questions.**

1 What is Hogmanay?

2 What are bagpipes?

3 Where is agriculture a school subject?

4 What language does Sesi's teacher speak?

5 When is carnival in Rio de Janeiro?

6 When does Carolina make her costume?

Pronunciation

-ing forms

3 🎧 **Listen to sentences 1–4. Do you hear a or b?**

	1	**a** speak	**b** speaking
	2	**a** play	**b** playing
	3	**a** wear	**b** wearing
	4	**a** dance	**b** dancing

4 🎧 **Listen and repeat the sentences in exercise 3.**

Exploring grammar

Present continuous: affirmative and negative

We use the present continuous to talk about actions in progress at the time of speaking.

5 **Look at the texts on page 50 and complete the chart.**

Affirmative		
I	'm	
You / We / They	're	relaxing.
He / She / It	's	

Negative		
I	(1)	
You / We / They	(2)	relaxing.
He / She / It	(3)	

⬤ GRAMMAR · PAGE 118

6 **Check the spelling rules on page 119. Then write the -*ing* forms of these verbs.**

1	read	**5**	make	**9**	watch
2	write	**6**	do	**10**	celebrate
3	work	**7**	sleep		
4	swim	**8**	sit		

7 **Complete the text. Use the present continuous of the verbs in parentheses.**

Dream celebration

At my dream celebration, *I'm celebrating* (celebrate) my birthday in Rio. I (**1**) ...... (not wear) a costume. I (**2**) ...... (listen) to music and I (**3**) ...... (speak) to Shakira. We (**4**) .... (eat) Brazilian food and we (**5**) ...... (drink) exotic fruit juices. My friend Sarah is at the party. She (**6**) ...... (not eat). She (**7**) ...... (dance) with Ricky Martin.

8 **Write about your dream celebration. Use the verbs in the box.**

> celebrate   dance   speak   listen   eat   drink   wear

At my dream celebration, I'm celebrating ...

Position of adjectives

> **Adjectives come:**
>
> • after the verb *be*
> The music **is traditional**.
>
> • before a noun
> It's **traditional music**.

⬤ GRAMMAR · PAGE 119

9 **Put the words in order.**

watching / interesting / movie. / I'm / an
I'm watching an interesting movie.

1 It's / party! / a / great

2 costume. / She's / fantastic / a / wearing

3 happy / I'm / here. / very

4 listening to / We're / a / CD. / good

> ⬤ **Finished?**
>
> **Think of birthday presents for your friends.**
> *a CD for David*

Vocabulary

Clothes

1   **Check the meanings of words 1–10.**

1	sweatshirt	**6**	sweater
2	sneakers	**7**	hat
3	tracksuit	**8**	T-shirt
4	boots	**9**	skirt
5	jeans	**10**	belt

2   **Jamie is visiting Andy and Natalie in New Orleans. Make lists of their clothes.**

Jamie: boots

⬤ **VOCABULARY · PAGE 127**

3   **Write about your partner's clothes.**

Alicia is wearing ...

Andy   Jamie   Natalie

Listening

4   🎧 **It's the carnival. Listen to Jamie and Andy. Who are they looking for?**

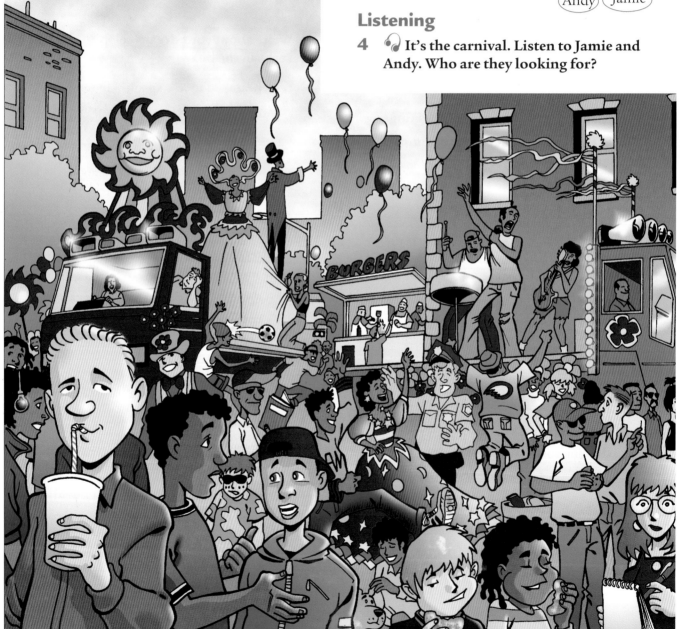

BURGERS

5 🎧 **Match questions 1–6 with answers a–f. Then listen again and check your answers.**

1b

1 Are you having fun?

2 What are they eating?

3 What instruments are they playing?

4 Is she playing an instrument?

5 Is she dancing?

6 Are your friends playing?

a No, she isn't.

b Yes, I am.

c The steel drums.

d King Cake.

e No, they aren't.

f Yes, she is.

Exploring grammar

Present continuous: questions

6 **Look at exercise 5. Complete the chart.**

Questions			
Am	I		
(1)	you we they		dancing?
(2)	he she it		
Short answers			
Yes,	I **am**. he / she / it **is**. we / you / they **are**.		
No,	I'm not. he / she / it **isn't**. we / you / they **aren't**.		

🔘 GRAMMAR • PAGE 118

7 **Put the words in order.**

singing? / Is / the man

Is the man singing?

1 What / are / eating? / the children

2 the woman / playing? / is / What instrument

3 wearing? / is / the man / What

4 the teenagers / wearing / jeans? / Are

5 is / What / the man / doing?

8 **Find the people from exercise 7 in the picture on page 52. Answer the questions from exercise 7.**

Is the man singing?   Yes, he is.

Speaking

9 **Work in pairs. Choose a person in the picture on page 52. Ask and answer questions and guess your partner's person.**

A: Is it a man or a woman?
B: A man.
A: Is he …

🔘 **Finished?**

Write about the people in the picture.
A woman is playing the guitar.

Study skills

Using a dictionary

In a dictionary, words are in alphabetical order.

1 Put the words in alphabetical order.

> cemetery   Pope   candy   Hindu   drum
> dead   marriage   dragon   pray

2 Check the order and meanings of
the words in a dictionary.

Listening

3 🎧 Look at photos 1–4 and listen to
commentaries a–c. Which celebrations
do you hear?

4 🎧 Listen again and answer the questions.

Commentary a

1 What is dancing through the streets?

2 What instrument are people playing?

Commentary b

3 How many people are there?

Commentary c

4 What time is it?

② **Easter Mass in the Vatican**

① **New Year's Eve in Times Square**

③ **The Day of the Dead in Mexico**

④ **Chinese New Year**

Reading

5 Are these sentences true or false?
Guess the answers.

1 People of all religions celebrate Christmas.

2 There is a celebration called The Day of the Dead in America.

6 Read the text and check your answers.

Special days

While you are reading this, people are celebrating a hundred different things: birthdays, marriages, festivals, and carnivals. But special days are not the same in every part of the world. Hindus, for example, don't celebrate Christmas.

In many places, there is a special day when people remember the dead. In Spain this is called "El Día de Todos los Santos" and it is on November 1st. The night before this date, on October 31st, people in the U.S. and the U.K. celebrate a festival called Halloween. Children wear costumes and play games and they eat candy.

In Mexico, there is a festival called the Day of the Dead on November 1st and 2nd. People go to the cemeteries. They dance, sing, and eat special bread and candy called *dulces de calavera*. They also play traditional instruments, normally flutes and drums. It's a big party!

Dulces de calavera

Look!

Ordinal numbers: dates

October 31st = October thirty-first

1st	first	11th	eleventh
2nd	second	12th	twelfth
3rd	third	13th	thirteenth
4th	fourth	14th	fourteenth
5th	fifth	15th	fifteenth
6th	sixth	20th	twentieth
7th	seventh	21st	twenty-first
8th	eighth	22nd	twenty-second
9th	ninth	30th	thirtieth
10th	tenth	31st	thirty-first

7 Complete the idea map. Use information from the third paragraph of the text.

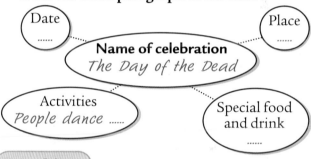

Speaking

8 Work in groups. Discuss the questions.

1 What celebrations are important in your country?

2 What are the dates of these celebrations?

3 What do you do on these special days?

Writing

Planning a paragraph

9 Choose a celebration in your country. Make an idea map.

10 Write a paragraph about your celebration.

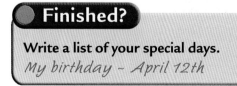

Finished?

Write a list of your special days.
My birthday ~ April 12th

Progress Check 5

Celebrations

1 Complete the names of the celebrations with the vowels *a, e, i, o,* and *u.*

C h r i s t m a s

1 H_ll_w__n
2 Th_nksg_v_ng
3 N_w Y__r's D_y
4 E_st_r
5 b_rthd_y
6 c_rn_v_l
7 V_l_nt_n_'s D_y

Clothes

2 Look at the picture of Christmas. Write the names of the clothes.

1 belt

Position of adjectives

3 Rewrite the sentences. Include the words in parentheses.

They eat *special* candy. (special)

1 That's a book. (big)
2 This is a party. (great)
3 She's wearing a T-shirt. (red)
4 Yes, he is. (good)

Present continuous: affirmative and negative

4 Complete the text about the picture of Christmas. Use the verbs in the box.

isn't listening   isn't eating   are playing
'm talking   is reading   is sleeping
're relaxing

Mark's Christmas

We *'re relaxing* after our Christmas dinner. My grandfather (**1**) ...... on the sofa, as usual, and my mother and father (**2**) ...... my new computer game. I (**3**) ...... to my father, but he (**4**) ...... to me. My sister Sue (**5**) ...... the TV guide. She (**6**) ...... her Christmas cake – the dog is eating it!

Present continuous: questions

5 Complete the questions about the picture of Christmas. Then answer the questions.

Mark / watch TV?

Is Mark watching TV? No, he isn't.

1 Sue / wear sneakers?
2 Mark's mother / eat cake?
3 Mark's parents / play a game?
4 Mark's grandfather / play a game?

6 Place to place

Take a look!

Find the pages where you:

- do a traffic and transportation survey.
- write about a school trip.
- read about a motorcycle adventure.

Vocabulary

The weather: adjectives

1 🎧 Listen and repeat the words in the box.

> cold hot sunny rainy windy
> cloudy wet dry

● VOCABULARY • PAGE 127

Speaking

2 **Work in pairs. Ask and answer the questions.**

1 What's the weather like today?
2 What weather do you like?
3 What's the weather like in your area in these months?

January   March   July   October

① cold

② rainy

③ sunny

④ wet

⑤ cloudy

⑥ windy

⑦ dry

⑧ hot

Reading

1 **Look at the photo and the title of the text. Answer the questions.**

1 Where does the woman plan to go?

2 What form of transportation does she prefer?

3 What do you think are the problems for travelers in the desert?

2 🎧 **Read and listen. Check your answers to exercise 1.**

Trans-Sahara

Stephanie Bates is a motorcycle fanatic. Every year she travels to a different part of the world on her motorcycle. Stephanie's favorite places are deserts, and this year she plans to cross the Sahara. Here she explains her preparation and some of the problems.

"Obviously, deserts aren't good for a motorcycle, and it's a long trip: my route is 4,000 kilometers. The weather is also a problem. It's often 45°C in the day, but it's very cold at night and you need some warm clothes. Sometimes it's very windy and you can't see. What do I take? Well, the basic things are a tent, maps, a compass, and some food and water. Oh, and some very good sunglasses. For emergencies you need some extra gasoline and tools for the motorcycle.

I also take one or two photos and some postcards – people are interested in them. I don't take any books with me, but I always take Sandy, my special teddy bear: you need some luck in the desert."

3 **Read the text again and answer the questions.**

1 How far is Stephanie's route?

2 What's the temperature in the day in the Sahara?

3 Does she take any warm clothes?

4 What does she take for emergencies?

5 Does she take any books?

6 What is Sandy?

Vocabulary

Things for a trip

4 **Look at the words in the box and the picture of Stephanie's things. Which three objects are not in the picture?**

> penknife   backpack   sleeping bag
> map   flashlight   sunglasses   tent
> batteries   matches   compass

● **VOCABULARY · PAGE 127**

Look!

Singular	Plural
backpack	backpack**s**
match	match**es**
battery	batter**ies**
compass	compass**es**
penknife	pen**knives**
person	**people**

● **GRAMMAR · PAGE 119**

Exploring grammar

some and *any*

6 Look at the examples and complete the rules with *some* and *any*.

Examples
You need **some** luck.
I don't take **any** books.
Does he take **any** warm clothes?

Rules
1 We use ...... in affirmative sentences.
2 We use ...... in negative sentences.
3 We use ...... in questions.

(GRAMMAR • PAGE 119)

7 Choose the correct word for each sentence.

I have **any** / (**some**) gasoline.

1 I don't need **some** / **any** money.

2 I don't have **some** / **any** matches.

3 Do you need **some** / **any** books?

4 I have **some** / **any** food.

Countable and uncountable nouns

Countable nouns
These nouns have singular and plural forms.
We use (1) **a** / **an** with singular forms.
We use (2) **some** / **any** with plural forms.

Uncountable nouns
These nouns don't have plural forms.
We use (3) **some** / **any** with these nouns.
We can't use (4) **a** / **an**.

(GRAMMAR • PAGE 119)

8 Look at the nouns in exercise 7. Are they countable or uncountable?

gasoline – *uncountable*

1 money   **3** books

2 matches   **4** food

9 🎧 Complete the dialog with *a*, *an*, *some*, and *any*. Then listen and check.

Sales clerk: Can I help you?

Meg: Yes, do you have *any* tents?

Sales clerk: Yes, we have (**1**) ...... excellent tents. Do you need (**2**) ...... sleeping bag?

Meg: No, I have (**3**) ...... old sleeping bag, but I need (**4**) ...... small flashlight and (**5**) ...... batteries.

Sales clerk: OK. Well, we have (**6**) ...... flashlights, but we don't have (**7**) ...... batteries right now. Sorry.

Pronunciation

/s/ + consonant

10 🎧 Listen and repeat.

1 small   **3** special

2 Stephanie   **4** sleeping bag

11 🎧 Listen and repeat.

Stephanie has a **sp**ecial **sm**all **sl**eeping bag.

Speaking

12 Write and practice a shopping dialog. Use words from exercise 4 and sentences from exercise 9.

Finished?

Make a list of things for a trip to Alaska.

dictionary, warm clothes, ...

Vocabulary

Forms of transportation

1 🎧 Listen and repeat words 1–8.

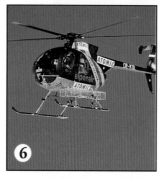

2 🎧 Listen to the sounds. Write the form of transportation you hear.

(VOCABULARY • PAGE 127)

Listening

3 🎧 Read the introduction to Louise's survey. Then listen and write Paul's answers.

Traffic and transportation survey

In our town there are some buses, but there aren't any trains. Some people bike, but a lot of people usually travel by car. And there is a lot of traffic! I am doing a survey in our class to find out some facts.

1 How do you normally travel to school?
a By car. **c** By bus.
b On foot. **d** Other.

2 Is there a lot of traffic near your home?
a Yes, there is.
b No, there isn't.

3 Are there any dangerous roads near your home?
a Yes, there are.
b No, there aren't.

4 Do you wear a helmet when you bike?
a Yes, I do.
b No, I don't.

5 Are there any bus stops near your home?
a Yes, there are.
b No, there aren't.

Look!

by and **on**

by car, train, bike, train

on foot

(GRAMMAR • PAGE 120)

Exploring grammar

there is / there are

4 Look at the survey on page 60. Complete the chart.

Affirmative		
There	(1)	a lot of traffic.
	(2)	some buses.

Negative		
There	isn't	an airport.
	(3)	any trains.

Questions		
(4)	there	a lot of traffic.
(5)		any dangerous roads?

Short answers

Yes, there is. / No, there isn't.
Yes, there are. / No, there aren't.

(GRAMMAR • PAGE 120)

5 🎧 Complete the results of Louise's survey. Use *is*, *are*, *isn't*, and *aren't*. Then listen and check.

In my group ...

- there (**1**) ...... three people who travel by car.
- there (**2**) .... one person who goes on foot.
- there (**3**) ...... any bus stops near people's homes.
- two people wear a helmet when they bike.
- there (**4**) ...... dangerous roads near three people's homes.
- there (**5**) .... a lot of traffic near two people's homes.

Speaking

6 In groups of four, do the traffic and transportation survey on page 60.

7 Write the results of your survey. Use the sentences in exercise 5. Then compare your results with the other groups.

In our group, there is one person who travels by bus.

8 Look at the information about Louise and Paul's town. Write sentences about the places.

Our town			
Stores	✓	Restaurants	✓
Sports center	✗	Movie theater	✗
Internet café	✗	Games arcade	✓
Swimming pool	✗	Nightclubs	✗

There are some stores.

There isn't a sports center.

9 Write sentences about your town.

There are two Internet cafés.

There aren't any movie theaters.

Finished?

Draw a diagram to illustrate one of your survey results.

Listening

1 🎧 **Listen to the dialog. Who gets up at six o'clock?**

> Mary   Linda

2 🎧 **Read the sentences about Mary. Put sentences a–f in order. Then listen and check.**

1 f

a She finds a flashlight.

b She goes out of the tent.

c She finds water in the tent.

d She looks for batteries.

e She looks for her clothes.

f She hears a mosquito.

Reading

3 **Read the letter and answer the questions.**

1 Is there a swimming pool at the campground?

2 What's the weather like?

3 What time does the nightclub close?

4 What do Mary and Linda do during the day?

5 What do they do in the evenings?

6 What is Linda's problem?

> Happy Valley Campground,
> Monterey,
> California.
> April 12th
>
> Dear Dave,
>
> I'm writing to you from our campground in California. We're here on a school trip, and I'm having a great time. There's always something to do. The campground is good. It has a store, a café, and a swimming pool.
>
> The weather is wet and windy, but it doesn't matter. We go somewhere different every day. We walk or go by bike. In the evening, we play table tennis or we go to town by bus with one of the teachers. There's sometimes a dance at the campground, but it's not great, and it finishes at 9:30.
>
> The only problem here is Mary! I'm sharing a tent with her, but she hates camping. She doesn't sleep at night, and she gets up at six o'clock in the morning, when I'm sleeping. She doesn't like anyone here, and she doesn't want to do anything. Ugh!
>
> Someone's calling me – it's lunchtime.
> How are things with you? Write soon.
> Sincerely,
> Linda

Writing

An informal letter

4 Look at Linda's letter. Complete the chart.

Place:	Happy Valley Campground, *Monterey*
Date:	...... (**1**)
Start of the letter:	(**2**) ...... Dave,
End of the letter:	(**3**) ...... , Linda

5 Look at photos a–c and choose a place for your school trip.

6 Write a letter to a friend from place a, b, or c. Include this information:

- Where are you?
- Are you with anyone?
- What's the weather like?
- Is there anything to do in the day?
- Is there anything to do in the evening?

a) Skiing in Vail

b) Disney World, Florida

c) Safari in Africa

● **Finished?**

Imagine that some people are visiting your country for a week. Prepare an itinerary for them.

Monday – travel to theme park by bus.
Tuesday – ...

Progress Check 6

The weather: adjectives

1 Complete the adjectives.

1 c _ _ _ _ _ 　　　2 s _ _ _ _

3 w _ _ _ _ 　　　4 r _ _ _ _

Things for a trip

2 Match the words in the box with pictures 1–6.

> map　matches　compass　flashlight
> backpack　penknife

Means of transportation

3 Put the letters in order.

1 ichiteorepl　　4 hips

2 lnpae　　5 atirn

3 kibe　　6 rctoyemolc

Countable and uncountable nouns

4 Look at the words. Which three nouns are uncountable?

1 food　　4 problem

2 desert　　5 bus

3 water　　6 paper

some and any

5 Complete the dialog with some and any.

There are *some* people in that tent.

Stop! I don't have **(1)** ...... clothes.

Does he have **(2)** ...... money?

No, but he has **(3)** ...... tickets for the movies.

Excuse me, do you have **(4)** ...... bananas?

No, sorry, but we have **(5)** ...... hot dogs.

AT THE MOVIE THEATER...

there is / there are

6 Complete the dialog with the correct forms of *there is* and *there are*.

A: Excuse me, *are there* any trains to Seattle from here?

B: No, sorry, **(1)** .... But **(2)** ...... a bus.

A: **(3)** ...... a bus to Seattle from here?

B: Yes, **(4)** .... **(5)** ...... a bus every Sunday.

The World of English 3

Brook Park
(pages 66 and 67)

Review: present continuous

Function: Making arrangements

1   Who's speaking to Viki?

Culture File
(pages 68 and 69)

Topic: Clubs for young people

2   What is the name of this organization?

The World of Pop (page 70)

Artist: Gloria Estefan

Country: Cuba

Song: You'll be mine (party time)

3   What is the sun doing in Gloria's song?

Brook Park

See you at the youth club!

Sally Hey, Paul, what are you doing this evening?

Paul Nothing special. Why?

Sally Viki and I are going to the youth club at about six. Do you want to come?

Paul Sure. OK. Great. See you there.

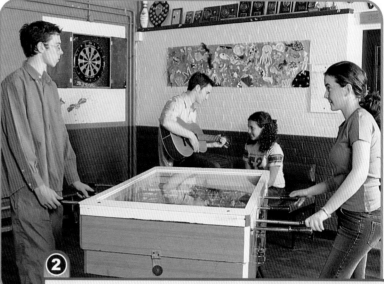

Paul Hi, Sally. Are you having fun? Who's talking to Viki?

Sally It's Calvin. Calvin Turner. You know, he's in tenth grade.

Paul Oh, yeah. He's a real know-it-all.

Sally Is not! His band is really good, and Viki likes him.

Paul What! You're joking!

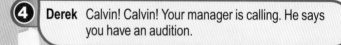

Derek Calvin! Calvin! Your manager is calling. He says you have an audition.

Viki What do you think of Calvin?

Paul Ooh, my ears! This music is awful!

Sally You're just jealous, Paul.

Paul Jealous? Ha! I have an idea. What's the youth club phone number?

Paul Wow. Is that Viki playing the guitar? I'm impressed.

Sally Me too, but Calvin isn't impressed with you. Look!

Paul Actually, I'm late. See you later, Sally.

Reading

1 🎧 Read and listen to Brook Park episode 3 again. Then answer the questions.

1. Where and when does Paul meet Sally?
2. Who is Viki talking to?
3. Does Paul like Calvin's music?
4. Who calls Calvin?
5. What does Paul think about Viki's playing?

Useful expressions

2 Find the expressions in the story and check their meaning.

1. Are you having fun?
2. You're joking!
3. I'm impressed.
4. Me too.

Dialog

Making arrangements

3 🎧 Look at this extract from Brook Park episode 3. Listen and repeat. Concentrate on your rhythm and intonation.

A: Hey, Paul, what are you doing this evening?

B: Nothing special. Why?

A: Viki and I are going to the youth club at about six. Do you want to come?

B: Sure. OK. Great. See you there.

4 Imagine that you want to go somewhere this weekend. Answer the questions.

1. Who are you going with?
2. Who do you want to invite?
3. Where are you going?
4. When are you going?

5 In groups of three, discuss your ideas from exercise 4. Use the dialog in exercise 3 as a model. Substitute the blue words to make your own dialogs.

> A: Hey, Daniel, what are you doing this evening?
>
> B: Nothing special. Why?
>
> A: Karina and I are going to the sports center at about five. Do you want to come?
>
> B: Sure. OK. Great. See you there.

Culture File 3

Clubs for young people

1 **Work in pairs. Discuss the questions.**

   1 Are you a member of any clubs or organizations?

   2 How often do you meet?

   3 What activities do you do?

2 **Read the text and look at the photo. Do you have a similar organization in your country?**

3 **Read the text again and answer the questions.**

   How many members does the BSA have?

   It has approximately five million members.

   1 How old are Boy Scouts?

   2 Are Scoutmasters adults or children?

   3 What skills do Scouts learn?

   4 How many Boy Scout ranks are there?

   5 How does a Boy Scout earn a merit badge?

   6 What is the top Boy Scout rank?

   7 When do Scouts meet?

   8 What activities do Scouts do at summer camp?

4 **Look at the list of the survival skills that Scouts learn. How many of these can you do?**

Boy Scouts of America

The Boy Scouts of America (BSA) is a very popular organization in the United States, with approximately five million members. This includes Cub Scouts (aged 6–10), Boy Scouts (aged 11–18), Scoutmasters and other adult helpers.

There are Scout clubs in every city and town. Scouts do a lot of outdoor activities and they learn survival skills. For example, all Scouts learn how to:

- **use camping equipment**
- **do basic first aid**
- **use a map and compass**
- **make a fire**
- **cook over a campfire**
- **swim**

Scouts wear uniforms and they are divided into groups called patrols. Each patrol has a leader. There are six Boy Scout levels, or ranks. When a Boy Scout learns a new skill and finishes a project, he earns a merit badge. He wears this badge on his uniform. Patrol members often earn their badges together. When a Boy Scout has the correct number of merit badges, he moves to the next rank. Eagle Scout is the top rank and it needs 21 merit badges. Every Boy Scout's dream is to be an Eagle Scout.

Scout troops usually meet every week. On weekends they sometimes go on camping trips. This is an opportunity to practice their skills. In the summer, Scouts can spend a week at a Scout summer camp, where they do all their favorite outdoor activities – swimming, fishing, kayaking, and climbing.

5 Look at the photos. What are the people doing?

1   They are eating and drinking.

6 🎧 Listen to Jenny talking about her Teen Center activities. Complete the fact sheet.

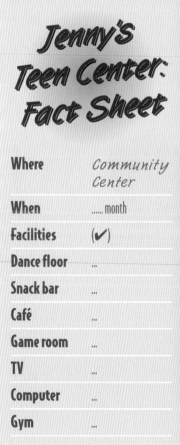

Jenny's Teen Center: Fact Sheet

Where	Community Center
When	...... month
Facilities	(✔)
Dance floor	...
Snack bar	...
Café	...
Game room	...
TV	...
Computer	...
Gym	...

7 Listen again. Are the sentences true or false?

Jenny is fifteen years old. *False*

1   Jenny enjoys dancing at the Teen Center.
2   There are video games at the Teen Center.
3   Jenny isn't very good at table tennis.
4   There is a computer at the Teen Center.
5   Parents come to the Teen Center.
6   Baseball is popular at the Teen Center.

8 Complete the table. Are the activities from Scouting or the Teen Center?

1   Swimming   *Scouting*
2   Dancing
3   Camping
4   Playing table tennis

🔴 Project

Make a poster to advertise your ideal club. Think about these things:

- Where is it?
- When is it?
- Who goes?
- What happens there?

Decorate your poster with drawings or with pictures from magazines.

The World of Pop 3

Gloria Estefan

Name: Gloria Estefan

Date of birth: September 1st, 1957

Place of birth: Havana, Cuba

Present home: Miami, U.S.

Education: University of Miami (Psychology)

Family: husband (Emilio) and two children (Nayib and Emily Marie)

You'll be mine (party time)

(Chorus)
1 When the sun is setting in the *sky*.
2 Everybody knows it's party time,
3 And when the moon is rising (**1**) ......
4 I am yours, I know you are (**2**) ...... (party time).

5 All day the world goes round and (**3**) ......
6 You can feel the changes coming down.
7 It doesn't matter who you are
8 With love to give you can go (**4**) ......
9 We see the treasures all around
10 And burn ourselves into the ground.
11 Everyone's trying to (**5**) ......
12 We're not just born to be alive.

13 I know
14 What I feel inside is (**6**) ......
15 You know
16 Every road I follow's leading me to (**7**) ......

(Repeat chorus)

17 We live our lives in mystery
18 While everything is meant to be.
19 No reason here to wonder (**8**) ...... –
20 All that we seek is in the sky.
21 You are the one that I want to hold;
22 I feel you deep inside my soul.
23 Only our love will set us (**9**) ...... –
24 This night belongs to you and me.

Gloria Estefan (Cuba)

1 **Look at the information about Gloria Estefan. Answer the questions.**

1 How old is Gloria now?

2 Where is she from?

3 Where does she live now?

4 What's her husband's name?

2 **Complete the song with the words in the box.**

> true   mine   high   survive   why
> round   you   far   sky   free

3 🎧 **Listen to the song and check your answers.**

4 **Find lines in the song with the same meanings as sentences 1–4. Choose a or b for each sentence.**

1 The world never stops.

  a line 5   **b** line 16

2 Love is important.

  a line 14   **b** line 8

3 There are fantastic things in life.

  a line 9   **b** line 16

4 We don't understand what's happening.

  a line 17   **b** line 22

Glossary

7 It doesn't matter = It isn't important

12 just = simply

7 Survive

Take a look!

Find the pages where you:

- listen to an interview with two Aborigines.
- read about animal survival.
- read about survival in the jungle.

Vocabulary

Animals

1 Match the words in the box with animals 1–6 in the picture. Which animals in the box are not in the picture?

> butterfly snake frog crocodile parrot
> penguin mosquito fish chameleon spider

2 🎧 Listen and repeat the words in exercise 1.

3 Which animals in exercise 1 live in your country?

⬤ VOCABULARY • PAGE 128

Vocabulary

Skills

1 🎧 Match the skills with pictures 1–6. Then listen and repeat.

> hunt   play an instrument   make a fire
> sew   cook   speak a language

⬤ VOCABULARY · PAGE 128

Listening

2 🎧 Listen to *The survival program.* Are the sentences true or false? Correct the false sentences.

> Lewis can play the didgeridoo.
>
> *False. Lewis can't play the didgeridoo.*

1 Jim and Lewis can speak the Aborigine language.

2 Jim can use a computer.

3 Jim can't make a fire.

4 Lewis can't make a fire.

5 Jim can sew.

7:00 The survival program

Jim and his grandson Lewis talk about the survival of traditional skills in the Aborigine community.

Exploring grammar

can

3 Complete the chart.

Affirmative		
Jim	**can**	cook.

Negative		
Jim	(1)	use a computer.

Questions		
(2)	Jim	cook?

Short answers
Yes, I / you / he / she / it / we / they (3) ....
No, I / you / he / she / it / we / they (4) ....

GRAMMAR · PAGE 120

4 Choose the correct verb forms.

Jim (can) / can't play the didgeridoo.

1 I **can** / **can't** make a fire.

2 Jim and Lewis **can** / **can't** speak English.

3 I **can** / **can't** use a computer.

4 Lewis **can** / **can't** use a computer.

5 I **can** / **can't** dance.

5 Put the words in order.

you / Can / the guitar? / play

Can you play the guitar?

1 read / Can / you / a map?

2 run / three kilometers? / you / Can

3 Can / a computer? / you / use

4 you / Can / two languages? / speak

5 play / you / chess? / Can

Pronunciation

Weak forms: *can*

6 🎧 Listen and repeat.

a can /kæn/   **b** can /kən/

7 🎧 Listen to sentences 1–3. Do you hear a or b?

1 Can you cook?   2 Yes, I can.

3 I can swim.

8 🎧 Listen and write the sentences.

Speaking

9 In pairs, ask and answer the questions in exercise 5.

10 In pairs, ask and answer about these activities. Use *Can you ...* and the words in the box.

cook   sew   play volleyball   make a fire
~~play the piano~~   speak French
swim 25 meters

A: *Can you play the piano?*
B: *Yes, I can. / No, I can't.*

Finished?

Write some sentences about your partner.
Raquel can play the piano.

Reading

1 Guess the answers to the questions.

1 What do you need in the jungle?

2 What food can you find in the jungle?

3 Where can you find water in the jungle?

4 What jungle animals are dangerous?

2 🎧 Read and listen. Check your answers.

3 Read the text again and complete the sentences.

1 ...... maps, a compass, a good knife ......

2 ...... a good insect repellent.

3 ...... a shelter and a fire.

4 ...... for water in plants.

5 You should ...... insects for ten minutes.

6 You shouldn't ...... strange plants.

Survival in the jungle

You need four things to survive in the jungle: water, food, shelter, and fire. Forget your CD player and your best sneakers. Take maps, a compass, a good knife, and walking boots.

Animals can be a problem, particularly spiders, snakes, and mosquitoes. But don't panic! Use a good insect repellent. Remember: when you get up you should always look for insects and spiders in your clothes and boots.

Make a shelter and a fire before it gets dark. And always sleep near the fire. You can stay warm and big animals don't like the light.

It isn't difficult to find food and water in the jungle. Look for water in rivers or plants. Rivers are sometimes contaminated and you should sterilize water before you drink it. And be careful: crocodiles live in big rivers.

If you don't have any food, you can eat fruit or some insects, but remember: you should cook insects for a minimum of ten minutes, and you shouldn't eat strange plants.

Look!

Imperatives

Forget your CD player.

Don't panic.

Be careful.

🔵 **GRAMMAR • PAGE 121**

Exploring grammar

should

4 **Look at the text on page 74 and complete the examples.**

> ### Examples
>
> You (1) ...... cook insects for ten minutes.
> You (2) ...... eat strange plants.
>
> ### Rule
>
> We use **should** and **shouldn't** for obligation or advice.

🔵 **GRAMMAR • PAGE 121**

5 **What should you do in the jungle? Choose the correct verb forms.**

You (should) / shouldn't remember your maps.

1 You **should** / **shouldn't** use an insect repellent.
2 You **should** / **shouldn't** make a fire at night.
3 You **should** / **shouldn't** go near crocodiles.
4 You **should** / **shouldn't** drink contaminated water.
5 You **should** / **shouldn't** wear good boots.

6 **Write rules for the signs. Use *You should* and *You shouldn't* and the words in the box.**

> play soccer   drink   ~~go in~~   bike
> be careful   stop

You shouldn't go in.

①

②

③

④

⑤

Prepositions of place

7 **Check the meaning of the prepositions.**

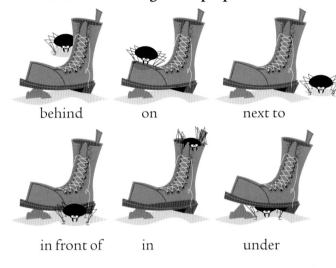

behind   on   next to

in front of   in   under

🔵 **GRAMMAR • PAGE 121**

8 **Write sentences with prepositions.**

parrot / table
The parrot is on the table.

1 spider / map
2 boots / table
3 butterflies / backpack

4 snake / backpack
5 parrot / map
6 map / table

> 🔵 **Finished?**
>
> **Make signs for these rules.**
>
> 1 You shouldn't smoke.
> 2 Don't touch the animals.
> 3 You should wear your bike helmet.
> 4 Don't use cell phones here.

Reading

1 **Read the text and choose a heading a–d for paragraphs 1–4.**

- Food
- What animals need
- Water
- Protection

2 **Read the text again. Answer the questions.**

1 What three things do animals need to find?
2 How long can camels live without water?
3 What does the Emperor penguin hunt?
4 What can it do?
5 What type of animal is a sea eagle?
6 What is special about the sea eagle?
7 Why is color important for animals?
8 Name two animals that use camouflage.

Adapt and survive

1 ....

To survive, animals adapt to their habitat, to the place where they live. They need to find food, water, and protection. The animal world is interesting because animals adapt in different ways.

2 ....

In some places this is very difficult. In the desert, for example, there isn't a lot of water, so animals conserve liquid in their bodies. Camels in Africa can survive seven days without water or food. Most other animals need water every day to survive.

3 ....

The Emperor penguin also lives in an extreme climate. This Antarctic bird hunts fish. It can't fly, but it can swim 45 kilometers an hour and it can survive temperatures of minus 40 degrees centigrade. The sea eagle is another bird that hunts fish. This bird can fly and see fish from a distance of three kilometers.

4 ....

Color is very important in the animal world, and some animals are the same color as their environment. This helps them escape predators or hunt more efficiently. For example, animals that live in snowy areas, like the polar bear, are often white. The chameleon is an expert in camouflage. It can change the color of its skin. Other animals, like butterflies and crocodiles, imitate natural objects.

Listening

3 Look at photos a–c and the chart. Guess the missing information.

4 🎧 Listen to a program about Australia's dangerous animals. Check your answers.

	a Taipan	**b** Crocodile	**c** Redback spider
Size	2·5 meters	3 to (**3**) ...... meters	(**7**) ...... centimeters
Habitat	farms	coast and (**4**)	near houses
Food	rats and mice	(**5**) ......, birds, and animals	(**8**) ......
Poisonous?	(**1**)	(**6**)	yes
Dangerous to humans?	(**2**)	yes	(**9**) ......

Writing

Planning an essay

5 Look at the essay plan and the information about mosquitoes. Match points 1–5 in the plan with the information in a–e.

> Dangerous animals – essay plan
>
> 1 Description (color, size, weight)
>
> 2 Habitat (countries, places)
>
> 3 Diet
>
> 4 Poisonous?
>
> 5 Dangerous to humans?

a They are common in all countries. They usually live near water.

b They are a serious problem in some countries.

c They aren't poisonous, but they can cause disease.

d They drink the blood of other animals.

e Mosquitoes are usually black and grey. They are between 4mm and 1.5cm long.

6 Find information about a different dangerous animal and write an essay. Use the essay plan in exercise 5.

Study skills

Finding information

You can find information for your schoolwork in different places.

7 Complete the words.

1 ency......   2 Int......   3 mag......

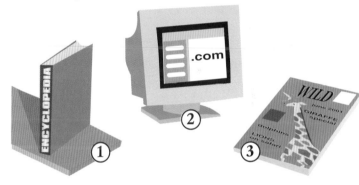

8 Think of more places where you can find information. Make a list.

1 TV

9 Which of the places in exercise 7 and 8 do you use?

● Finished?

Find eight words for parts of different animal's bodies. Illustrate your words.

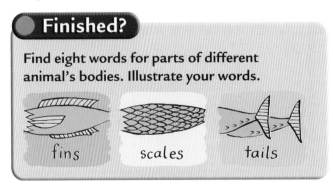

fins   scales   tails

Progress Check 7

Animals

1 Complete the words.

cro *codile*

1 cha ......
2 sna ......
3 spi ......
4 fi ......
5 fr ......
6 par ......
7 pen ......

Skills

2 Match the words in the box with pictures 1–5.

sew~~ speak a language hunt
play an instrument make a fire

1 sew

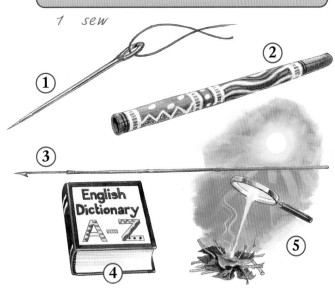

can

3 Make questions with *can*. Then answer the questions.

Test your animal knowledge!

1 ... monkeys speak English?
2 ... snakes move at 100 kilometers an hour?
3 ... spiders fly?
4 ... penguins change color?
5 ... crocodiles swim?

should

4 Complete the sentences with *You should* or *You shouldn't*.

Survival in the desert

You should **make a fire at night.**

1 ... drink a lot of water.
2 ... travel alone.
3 ... protect your skin and eyes from the sun.
4 ... touch snakes or scorpions.

Prepositions of place

5 Where's the butterfly? Complete the phrases with prepositions of place.

1 *behind* the jar
2 ...... the jar
3 ...... the jar
4 ...... the jar
5 ...... the jar

8 Home

Take a look!

Find the pages where you:

- answer questions in a computer game.
- listen to a dialog between neighbors.
- read a magazine article.

Vocabulary

Furniture

1 Match the words in the box with objects 1–8 in the picture. Which objects in the box are not in the picture?

> shelf   desk   lamp   light   cupboard
> mirror   stereo   bed   closet
> night table

2 🎧 Listen and repeat the words in exercise 1.

Speaking

3 Work in pairs. Ask and answer questions about your room.

> A: Do you have a stereo in your room?
> B: No, I don't.

VOCABULARY · PAGE 128

Reading

1 🎧 **Read and listen. Then look at pictures a and b. Which is Michael's new room?**

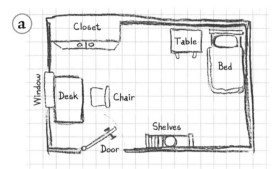

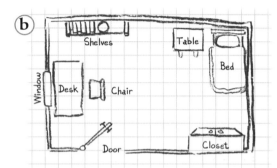

2 **Read the text again. Are the sentences true or false?**

1 Michael's parents are going to give him $1,000.

2 Michael can use the money for CDs.

3 His father is going to help Michael decorate.

4 His parents like all of his ideas.

5 Michael needs a new closet.

6 He isn't going to move his bed.

7 Michael isn't going to buy posters of pop stars.

8 He likes basketball and car racing.

Look!

Articles

a desk

an Angels fan

the room

◯ GRAMMAR · PAGE 122

Top Teen special
Change your room!

Does your room need a new look? Every week we're going to give $1,000 to one of our readers for paint, posters, pictures, and furniture. This week's winner is Michael Wade. Here Michael talks about his plans for his new room.

Top Teen What are your plans for your room?

Michael Well, first I'm going to paint the walls. My dad's going to help me. He says that I can change the color. Right now it's yellow, but I prefer red and white.

Top Teen Wow! What do your parents think?

Michael Well, they're going to think about it! Red is my favorite color. I'm an Angels fan and red and white are their colors.

Top Teen What about furniture?

Michael Well, I want a desk, and I need some shelves for my stereo and CDs. I'm not going to move my bed. The shelves can go next to the door, and I'm going to put the desk under the window.

Top Teen Anything else?

Michael Yes. I'm into car racing, and I'm going to buy a big picture of a Ferrari for the wall next to my bed.

Top Teen That's an excellent idea. Good luck, Michael!

Michael Thanks, and thanks again for the money.

Pronunciation

/ɪ/ and /i/

3 🎧 **Listen to the words.**

/ɪ/ give, picture, think

/i/ need, read, week

4 🎧 **Listen to sentences 1–3. Do you hear a or b?**

1	**a**	leave	**b**	live
2	**a**	sheep	**b**	ship
3	**a**	eat	**b**	it

5 🎧 **Listen and repeat the words in exercise 4.**

Exploring grammar

be going to: affirmative and negative

We use *be* + *going to* + infinitive when we speak about plans and intentions for the future.

6 **Complete the chart with** *isn't*, *not*, **and** *aren't*.

Affirmative	
I'm	
He / She / It**'s**	**going to** buy a TV.
We / You / They**'re**	
Negative	
I'm (1)	
He / She / It (2)	**going to** buy a TV.
We / You / They (3)	

(● **GRAMMAR · PAGE 121**)

7 **Complete the text with the affirmative and negative forms of** *be going to*.

Last week's *Top Teen* winner: Linda Harper

She*'s going to paint* (paint) her room light green. Her friends **(1)** ...... (help) her. Her parents **(2)** ...... (give) her a TV. She **(3)** ...... (not move) the furniture. She **(4)** ...... (not buy) any pictures. She **(5)** ...... (buy) a lamp and a mirror.

8 **Look at the table. Write sentences about Michael's and Linda's plans. Use affirmative and negative forms of** *be going to*.

Michael is going to buy a poster.

	Michael	**Linda**
have a TV in the room	No	Yes
buy a poster	Yes	No
paint their rooms	Yes	Yes
move the furniture	No	No

1 Michael ...... TV in the room.

2 Linda ...... TV in the room.

3 Linda ...... buy a poster.

4 They ...... paint their rooms.

5 They ...... move the furniture.

9 **Imagine that you are going to decorate and furnish your classroom. Write sentences with** *be going to* **and the verbs in the box.**

paint   change   move   buy   help

have   look for

I'm going to buy a computer for every student.

Speaking

10 **Work in pairs. Compare your answers. Then tell the class your plans.**

We're going to decorate our classroom.

Finished?

Describe your ideal room.

Vocabulary

A house

1 🎧 **Match the words in the box with pictures 1–10. Then listen and repeat.**

> living room   yard   kitchen   bathroom
> office   dining room   attic   hallway
> bedroom   stairway

⬤ **VOCABULARY · PAGE 128**

Listening

2 🎧 **Listen to three dialogs and look at the picture. Match the people and the places.**

1	Mr. Smith	a	in the hallway
2	Zoe Platt	b	in the bedroom
3	Mrs. Smith	c	in the kitchen
4	Mrs. Platt	d	in the bathroom

Smith family   Platt family

3 🎧 **Answer the questions. Then listen again and check.**

1 Is Mr. Platt going to give the ball to Gary?

2 Who's he going to talk to?

3 What room are the Smiths going to decorate?

4 When are the Smiths going to go to Mexico?

5 Is Zoe Platt going to speak to Paul Smith?

6 Where are Zoe and Lucy going to study?

Exploring grammar

be going to: questions

4 **Complete the chart with *is* and *are*.**

Am	I	
(1)	he / she / it	going to speak?
(2)	we / you / they	

(GRAMMAR • PAGE 122)

5 **Look at Paul's and Zoe's plans. Put the words in order. Then answer the questions.**

	Paul	Zoe
Monday	Study	Study
Tuesday	Mom's birthday	Study
Wednesday	Study	Study
Thursday	Soccer practice	Study
Friday	Our party!	Violin practice

going to / on Friday? / Zoe / play the violin / Is

Is Zoe going to play the violin on Friday? Yes, she is.

1 Are / going to / Paul and Zoe /study / on Monday?

2 Study / Zoe / going to / Is / on Tuesday?

3 What / are / next Tuesday? / the Smiths / going to / celebrate

4 are / Paul and Gary / going to / When / have a party?

5 Zoe / a party? / going to / Is / have

6 🎧 **Complete the dialog with the words in the box. Then listen and check.**

(are   invite   ~~have~~   going   to   is)

Paul: Mom, is it OK if we *have* a party?

Mom: A party? Where are you going (1) ...... have a party?

Gary: In our house, in the living room.

Mom: Oh, yes? And who (2) ...... you going to invite?

Paul: Oh, some friends from school.

Mom: How many are you going to (3) ......?

Gary: Ten or twelve.

Mom: And what are you (4) ...... to eat?

Paul: Pizza, I suppose.

Mom: And who (5) ...... going to ask the neighbors?

Gary: Paul.

Paul: Gary.

Time expressions: future

We use time expressions to say when we are going to do something.

I'm going to study **this afternoon**.

7 **What's the date today? Write the dates for 1–4.**

1 tomorrow   3 next Monday

2 this weekend   4 next Friday

(GRAMMAR • PAGE 122)

8 **Write six sentences about your plans and intentions. Use the time expressions from exercise 7.**

Speaking

9 **Tell the class about your partner's plans.**

Tonight Marta is going to watch a movie.

Finished?

Write about your plans for the summer.

Mystery house

Reading

1 Read the clues in the computer game and answer the questions.

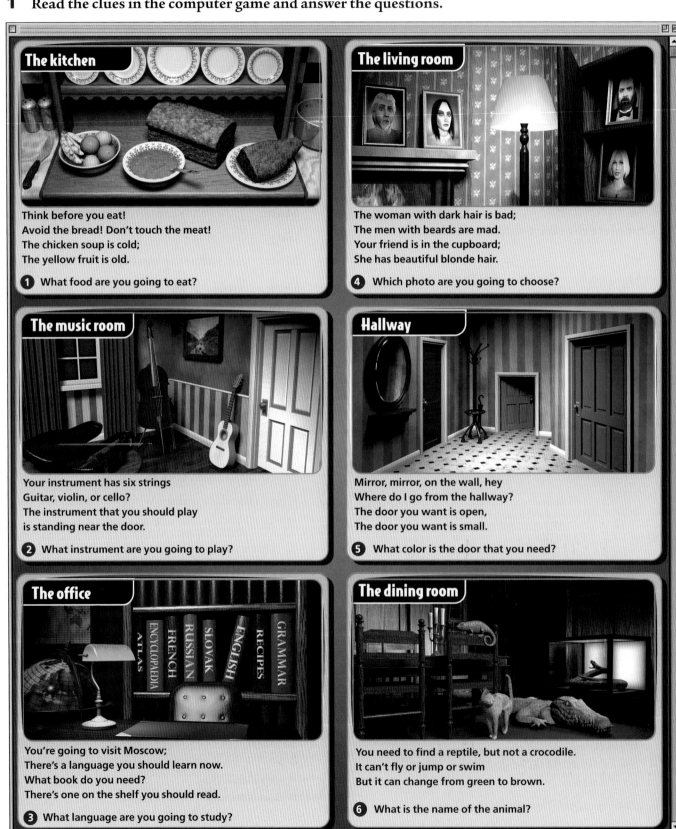

The kitchen

Think before you eat!
Avoid the bread! Don't touch the meat!
The chicken soup is cold;
The yellow fruit is old.

1 What food are you going to eat?

The living room

The woman with dark hair is bad;
The men with beards are mad.
Your friend is in the cupboard;
She has beautiful blonde hair.

4 Which photo are you going to choose?

The music room

Your instrument has six strings
Guitar, violin, or cello?
The instrument that you should play
is standing near the door.

2 What instrument are you going to play?

Hallway

Mirror, mirror, on the wall, hey
Where do I go from the hallway?
The door you want is open,
The door you want is small.

5 What color is the door that you need?

The office

ATLAS ENCYCLOPAEDIA FRENCH RUSSIAN SLOVAK ENGLISH RECIPES GRAMMAR

You're going to visit Moscow;
There's a language you should learn now.
What book do you need?
There's one on the shelf you should read.

3 What language are you going to study?

The dining room

You need to find a reptile, but not a crocodile.
It can't fly or jump or swim
But it can change from green to brown.

6 What is the name of the animal?

Speaking

2 Look at the opinions about computer games. Tell the class your opinion.

I think that they're fun.

They're fun.

They're bad for you.

You can learn things from them.

Some games are violent.

The price isn't important.

They're really expensive.

You stay in the house all day when you play computer games.

Listening

3 🎧 Peter is playing "Mystery house". Listen to the dialog between Peter and his mother. Is she interested in the game?

4 🎧 Listen again and answer the questions.

1 What time is it?
2 What's Peter going to buy tomorrow?
3 What does Peter's mother think about computer games?
4 What level of "Mystery house" is Peter playing?
5 What does Peter's mother want to see?

Writing

Giving reasons: *because*

We use the word **because** when we give reasons and causes.

You should go to bed because it's twelve-thirty.

5 Join the facts and reasons. Use *because*.

Facts

1 Peter doesn't want to go to bed ...
2 Peter wants some money ...
3 Peter's mom doesn't like computer games ...
4 The questions are easy ...

Reasons

a ... he's going to buy a new game.
b ... it's Saturday tomorrow.
c ... this is level one.
d ... she thinks that they're expensive and violent.

6 Write your friend's opinions about computer games. Use *because* and ideas from exercise 2.

Daniela doesn't like computer games because she thinks that they're bad for you.

Gabriel likes computer games because ...

Miguel doesn't buy computer games ...

Finished?

Write your opinion about your house.
I like my bedroom because the colors are nice.

Progress Check 8

Furniture

1 **Write the names of objects 1–6.**

1 ......   4 ......

2 ......   5 ......

3 ......   6 ......

A house

2 **Complete the sentences.**

1 I sleep in my ......

2 We cook in the ......

3 We all watch TV in the ......

4 We eat in the ......

5 I take a shower in the ......

Time expressions: future

3 **Write a suitable time expression.**

When are you going to ...
have your next exam? *Next Thursday.*

1 do your English homework?

2 visit your grandparents?

3 go on vacation?

4 have a party?

be going to: affirmative and negative

In the U.S. some people are now buying old airplanes, and they're living in them!

Millionaire JJ Pinches and his wife Marina want to live in a plane.

4 **Complete the sentences with the affirmative or negative form of *be going to*.**

JJ *is going to buy* (buy) an old plane.

1 He ...... (not travel) on the plane.

2 He and his wife ...... (live) on the plane.

3 They ...... (move) next week.

4 They ...... (not decorate) the plane.

5 Some experts ...... (decorate) it.

be going to: questions

5 **Write questions with *be going to*.**

you / watch TV tonight?

Are you going to watch TV tonight?

1 you / take a shower?

2 What / you / do this weekend?

3 she / play tennis tomorrow?

4 Where / they / live?

5 John / play basketball next Saturday?

6 What time / you / get up tomorrow?

The World of English 4

Brook Park
(pages 88 and 89)

Review: *can, should, be going to*

Function: Making suggestions

1 What's Paul going to do?

Culture File
(pages 90 and 91)

Topic: Going out and staying in

2 Where is this place?

The World of Pop (page 92)

Artist: **Enrique Iglesias**

Country: **Spain**

Song: **Be with you**

3 Does Enrique live in Madrid?

Brook Park

Calvin's bad day

1

Paul	Well, what are we going to do? Do you have any ideas, Sally?
Sally	Yeah, let's go to the mall.
Paul	Mmm. Can we do something else? I know, why don't we go for a walk?
Viki	That's a good idea. Should we call Calvin?
Sally	Sure, why not?

2

Sally	Hey, nice scooter, Calvin! Do you have a driver's license now?
Calvin	A license? I'm not on the road, am I? Who's going to come for a ride?
Sally	Yeah, OK. Awesome!

3

Viki	Paul, look! Sally and Calvin are in trouble. Let's go! We should help them.
Paul	I'm going to call 911.

4

Calvin	Oooh, my leg! I can't stand up. Sally, are you OK?
Sally	I don't know. I can't move my hand.

5

Paramedic	Don't worry. Your friend is going to be fine, but I'm afraid the police are going to take your scooter.
Paul	Oh, man! Calvin's having a bad day.
Calvin	Stupid tree! I don't believe it! My parents are going to be furious!

Reading

1 🎧 **Read and listen to Brook Park episode 4 again. Then answer the questions.**

1 Where does Sally want to go?

2 What does Paul want to do?

3 What do Paul and Viki do when they see Calvin and Sally?

4 What are the police going to do with Calvin's scooter?

5 Who is going to be furious?

Useful expressions

2 **Find the expressions in the story and check their meaning.**

1 Awesome!   3 Let's go!

2 Nice scooter.   4 I don't believe it!

Dialog

Making suggestions

3 🎧 **Look at this extract from Brook Park episode 4. Listen and repeat. Concentrate on your rhythm and intonation.**

A: Well, what are we going to do? Do you have any ideas, Sally?

B: Yeah, let's go to the mall.

A: Mmm. Can we do something else? I know, why don't we go for a walk?

C: That's a good idea. Should we call Calvin?

B: Sure, why not?

4 **Look at the situations and think of ideas.**

1 You're bored.

2 A friend is sick in bed.

3 It's your friend's birthday.

4 You're planning a school trip.

April 11th

❀ Becky's ☆ Birthday ☆ ❀ 🎀

5 **In groups of three, discuss your ideas from exercise 4. Use the dialog in exercise 3 as a model. Substitute the blue words to make your own dialogs.**

A: Well, what are we going to do? Do you have any ideas, Paola?

B: Let's play basketball.

A: Mmm. Can we do something else? I know, why don't we go to the movies?

C: That's a good idea. Should we call Javier?

B: Sure, why not?

Culture File 4

Going out and staying in

1 Work in pairs. Discuss the questions.

1 What do you do when you go out?

2 What do you do when you stay in?

3 Which do you prefer?

2 Read the text. Who prefers going out and who prefers staying in?

Going out	Staying in
Roseanne	
(1)	(3) ......
(2)	(4) ......

3 Read the text again and answer the questions.

1 Who wants to be a TV announcer or director?
Leanne.

What are her favorite TV shows?

2 Who often falls off his skateboard?

Name two skateboarding rules.

3 Who goes to the mall with her friends?

What do she and her friends do at the mall?

4 Who likes reading?

What is she reading right now?

5 Who goes to a multiplex movie theater?

What is her other hobby?

"You have some free time ... do you stay in or go out?"
We asked this question to teenagers from North America and the U.K.

Roseanne is from Houston, U.S.

I go to the mall. It's all indoors so it's warm in winter and cool in summer. It has hundreds of stores and lots of snack bars and cafés. I usually go with friends. We go window shopping for clothes and CDs, and we have a drink or a snack. It's a great place to hang out on weekends and after school. It's open until 9:30 at night.

Steve is from London, England

There's a new skateboard park near my house and I go there a lot. I'm not very good and I often fall off my board, but I'm learning. Some of my friends can do amazing things. Skateboarding isn't dangerous, but you should follow the rules. You should wear a helmet and other protective equipment, and you should look out for other people, particularly beginners.

Beth is from Dundee, Scotland

I'm a bookworm – I stay in and read! I'm crazy about reading. When I'm in the middle of a good story, I can't stop. Sometimes I read all night, and then I'm very tired at school the next day. Right now, I'm reading Terry Pratchett's books. They're very exciting and funny.

Leanne is from Detroit, U.S.

I'm a TV addict – my favorite programs are DeGrassi and Smallville. We have over 150 channels, so there's always something to watch. My British pen pal only has five channels! Boring! In the future, I want to be a TV announcer or director.

Joey is from Halifax, Canada

I go out. There's a good multiplex movie theater in Halifax with ten screens. It usually has one or two movies I want to see. I'm also into online computer games with people all around the world. It's really exciting, but I still prefer spending my free time out of the house.

Mall of America

4 🎧 **Listen to Roseanne's report from the Mall of America. Match the numbers to the items.**

400   restaurants

14   visitors every year

42 million   college courses

37   stores

66   trees in The Park at MOA

530   movie theaters

5 🎧 **Listen to Roseanne again. Choose a or b.**

The Mall is a top tourist attraction, like …

a the Grand Canyon. **b** the U.S.

1 First, Roseanne is going to …

a go shopping. **b** visit The Park at MOA.

2 She's going to have lunch in …

a Bloomingdale's. **b** the Rainforest Café.

3 The Rainforest Café has …

a a zoo. **b** waterfalls.

4 The Park at MOA is a …

a theme park. **b** video game arcade.

5 You can get married at the …

a National American University.

b Chapel of Love.

6 **What should the teenagers from the reading do at Mall of America? Complete the table. Use the words in the box.**

> buy books   go to a sporting goods store
> see a movie   go window shopping
> look at the new TVs

1 Roseanne *should go window shopping.*

2 Joey …

3 Leanne …

4 Steve …

5 Beth …

Project

Do a class survey to find out what people in your class do in their free time.

Ask each student to write down their three favorite hobbies.

Draw a diagram to illustrate your results.

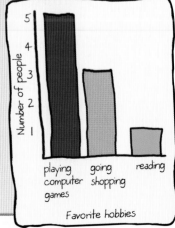

The World of Pop 4

Enrique Iglesias

Full name: Enrique Iglesias Preysler

Date of birth: May 8th, 1975

Place of birth: Madrid, Spain

Home town: Miami, U.S.

Brothers and sisters: Chabeli, Julio José

Likes: water sports, movies

Enrique Iglesias (Spain)

1 Read the information about Enrique Iglesias. Answer the questions.

  1 Where's Enrique from?

  2 How many brothers and sisters does he have?

  3 Where does he live now?

  4 What does he like?

2 Complete the song with the words in the box.

> sign smile slow life cold window
> sleep soul ~~low~~

3 🎵 Listen to the song and check your answers.

4 🎵 Listen again. Are the sentences true or false?

  1 The singer is very sad.

  2 He lives in the country.

  3 He wants to speak to his girlfriend.

  4 His girlfriend is with him.

  5 He can't imagine life without his girlfriend.

Be with you

1 Monday night, I feel so *low*,
2 Count the hours, they go so (**1**) ......
3 I know the sound of your voice
4 Can save my (**2**) ......
5 City lights, streets of gold,
6 Look out my (**3**) ...... to the world below,
7 Moves so fast and it feels so (**4**) ......
8 And I'm all alone.

9 Don't let me die –
10 I'm losing my mind.
11 Baby just give me a (**5**) ......

  (Chorus)
12 And now that you're gone
13 I just wanna be with you
14 And I can't go on.
15 I wanna be with you,
16 Wanna be with you.

17 I can't (**6**) ...... and I'm up all night.
18 Through these tears I try to (**7**) ......
19 I know the touch of your hand
20 Can save my (**8**) ......

21 Don't let me down,
22 Come to me now.
23 I got to be with you somehow.

  (Repeat chorus)

24 And now that you're gone
25 Am I without you now?
26 Ooh, I can't go on.
27 I just wanna be with you.

  (Repeat chorus)

Glossary

1 feel low = feel bad   21 let me down = disappoint me

10 losing my mind = going crazy   23 I got to = I need to

14 go on = continue

5 Think of advice for the person in the song.

He can talk to his friends.

He should try to be happy.

9 Fame

Take a look!

Find the pages where you:
- write a biography of a famous person.
- find out how to become famous.
- do a quiz about famous people.

Vocabulary

Famous people

1 🎧 Match the jobs with photos 1–9. Then listen and repeat.

composer artist businessperson
singer actor writer model
sports star scientist

2 Write lists of people for the jobs in exercise 1.

Composer: Mozart, ...

⬤ **VOCABULARY • PAGE 129**

P 49

Reading

1 Do the famous names quiz.

The famous names quiz

1 Bram Stoker was a writer from Ireland. What was the name of his famous book?

a Frankenstein
b Dracula
c Batman

2 In 2006 there was a famous movie called *Pirates of the Caribbean: Dead Man's Chest*. What is the name of the main actor in the movie?

a Johnny Depp
b Tom Hanks
c Bruce Willis

3 Salvador Dalí was an artist. Where was he from?

a Argentina
b Spain
c The United States

4 This person was a famous sports star in the 1990s. What's his name?

a Michael Jordan
b Jordan Michael
c Michael Schumacher

5 Beethoven and Bach were from Germany. Were they …

a … inventors?
b … composers?
c … artists?

6 J.K. Rowling is a British writer. Who was her famous creation?

a Jarvis Cocker
b Harry Potter
c Larry Cotter

7 Originally, there were four singers in this famous group. What was the name of the group?

a Destiny's Child
b Sugababes
c The Pussycat Dolls

8 This is Alexander Graham Bell. What was his famous invention?

a The telephone
b The car
c The lightbulb

Exploring grammar

was / were

2 **Look at the quiz. Copy and complete the chart with *was*, *were*, and *wasn't*.**

Affirmative and negative

I / He / She / It	*was* / (1)	famous.
We / You / They	(2) ...... / *weren't*	

Questions

(3)	I / he / she / it	famous?
Were	we / you / they	

(**GRAMMAR • PAGE 122**)

3 **Complete the text. Use *was*, *wasn't*, *were*, and *weren't*.**

John Lennon (1940–1980)

John Lennon *was* from Liverpool, England. At school, he was interested in art and music, but he (1) ...... a very good student. At 16, he (2) ...... in his first band, but they (3) ...... very popular. Four years later, John (4) ...... in a new band. Their music (5) ...... original and exciting, and they (6) ...... number one in the U.S. and the U.K. Their name? The Beatles!

4 **Complete the questions with *was* or *were*. Then answer the questions.**

Was Bram Stoker a singer?

No, he wasn't.

1 Where ...... Beethoven from?
2 ...... The Beatles inventors?
3 ...... Elvis Presley a writer?
4 When ...... the last soccer World Cup?
5 Where ...... the last Olympic games?

5 **Complete the dialog with *was*, *were*, and *wasn't*. Then listen and check.**

Tom: *Were* you at the movie theater with Paul yesterday?
Beth: Yes, I (1) ....
Tom: (2) ...... it a good movie?
Beth: The special effects (3) ...... excellent, but the story (4) ...... very good.
Tom: Who (5) ...... in it?
Beth: Johnny Depp and Keira Knightley.
Tom: (6) ...... they good?
Beth: Yes, they (7) .... All the actors (8) ...... good.

Speaking

6 **Look again at exercise 5. In pairs, make a dialog about a movie you know.**

Look!

there was / there were
There **was** a movie called *Shrek*.
There **were** five singers in this group.

(**GRAMMAR • PAGE 123**)

7 **Complete the sentences with *There was* and *There were*.**

1 ...... a good movie at the movie theater.
2 ...... some good actors in the movie.
3 ...... a terrible video on MTV.
4 ...... two really bad singers.
5 ...... a strange model on the video.

Finished?

Write about a movie you like.

Fame and fortune

Reading

1 Look at the people in the photos. What are their jobs and why are they famous?

2 🎧 Read and listen. Then check your answers.

3 Read the text again. Are the sentences true or false? Correct the false sentences.

1 Angelina Jolie studied in a normal school.

2 Picasso's work wasn't always popular.

3 Bill Gates' predictions weren't correct.

4 Talent scouts usually look for movie directors.

5 Gisèle Bündchen was a lucky discovery.

6 The Beatles were famous when they started.

Vocabulary

Regular verbs

The simple past of regular verbs ends in *-ed*.

4 Find the simple past of these verbs in the text.

start – *started*

1	study	5	discover
2	stop	6	work
3	criticize	7	travel
4	predict	8	play

⬤ VOCABULARY • PAGE 129

Pronunciation

Simple past *-ed*: /ɪd/

5 🎧 Listen and repeat. Which verb ends with the sound /ɪd/?

1 stopped 2 started 3 traveled

6 🎧 Listen and repeat. Which verb ends with the sound /ɪd/?

1	played	3	predicted
2	worked	4	discovered

⬤ GRAMMAR • PAGE 123

Do you want to be famous? *Top Teen* magazine has some advice: follow the five steps to fame.

1 Ambition
Be ambitious! A lot of famous people were ambitious when they were young. From the age of eleven, Angelina Jolie studied at a special "theater institute". She started to act in music videos when she was sixteen, and then she never stopped!

2 Vision
Be original! People with vision have original ideas, but their ideas aren't always popular. Picasso was a great painter, but people criticized his work. Businessman Bill Gates is now a billionaire, but when he predicted the computer boom, some people didn't listen.

3 Talent
Show your talent! There are talent competitions on TV, and talent "scouts" look for the stars of the future, especially in the worlds of music and sports. Talent scouts discovered soccer player Michael Owen when he was in school.

4 Luck
Knock on wood! Some stars worked hard to become famous. Others were very lucky. Brazilian supermodel Gisèle Bündchen was on vacation with her father when a model agent discovered her in a fast food restaurant. She was fourteen.

5 Energy
Work, work, work! Supergroup the Beatles didn't start at number 1. They worked and they traveled a lot. Sometimes they played three concerts in a day. The result: fame and fortune.

Exploring grammar

Simple past regular verbs: affirmative and negative

7 Look at the chart and complete the rule.

Affirmative	
I / You / He She / It / We They	worked.
Negative	
I / You / He She / It / We They	didn't work.

We form the negative of the simple past with ...... and the verb.

(GRAMMAR · PAGE 123)

8 Check the spelling rules on page 123. Then write the simple past affirmative forms of these verbs.

1 prefer 4 try 7 want

2 live 5 dance 8 stay

3 listen 6 practice 9 relax

(GRAMMAR · PAGE 123)

9 Think about your activities last weekend. Choose the correct form of the verbs.

I (biked) / didn't bike five kilometers.

1 I **listened** / **didn't listen** to a CD.

2 I **watched** / **didn't watch** TV.

3 I **studied** / **didn't study** English.

4 I **played** / **didn't play** tennis.

5 I **cooked** / **didn't cook** a meal.

6 I **danced** / **didn't dance** with my friends.

10 Complete the sentences about the picture. Use the words in the box.

study discover ~~wanted~~ started
studied didn't

He always *wanted* to be a star.

1 He ...... to play basketball when he was three.

2 The talent scouts didn't ...... him.

3 People ...... like his music.

4 He ...... drama.

5 He didn't ...... economics.

11 Write sentences about last week. Use the past simple of the verbs in the box.

watch listen to talk play study

On Saturday, I watched some music videos on MTV.

Look!

Prepositions of time

On Friday / Saturday morning / Sunday afternoon / Monday evening

Speaking

12 Work in groups of three. Tell each other about last week. Use other regular verbs.

On Monday evening, I stayed at my friend's house.

(Finished?)

Imagine that you are famous. Write some sentences about your life.

I started to sing when I was two.

Superstars

Reading

1 🎧 **Read and listen. Answer the questions about Christina Aguilera.**

1 When was she born?

2 How old was she when she first appeared on TV?

3 What did she do in 1994?

4 When did she sign her first record contract?

5 What was the title of Christina's first CD?

6 Was the record successful? How do you know?

7 What did she do between 2000 and 2005?

8 What are her plans for the future?

Look!

Years	
1479	fourteen seventy-nine
1998	nineteen ninety-eight
2000	two thousand
2003	two thousand and three
the 1990s	the nineteen nineties

Study skills

Word building

Some verbs and nouns are similar. It is easy to learn these words together.

2 **Complete the chart.**

Noun	Verb
dancer	*to dance*
actor	**(1)** ......
singer	**(2)** ......
performer	**(3)** ......

3 **Add these verbs to the chart. Write the nouns and then check your answers on page 129.**

1 to compose   3 to teach

2 to write   4 to model

🔵 VOCABULARY • PAGE 129

Christina Maria Aguilera was born in New York on December 18th, 1980. Her father is from Ecuador and her mother is from Ireland.

When she was young, Christina always wanted to be a star. At the age of eight, she appeared in a talent show on American TV, and in 1992 she started her professional career in a TV show called *The New Mickey Mouse Club.*

In 1994, the show finished and Christina decided to concentrate on music. She traveled a lot and performed in different countries, including Japan and Romania. Christina wanted to finish her first CD before she finished school.

In early 1998, she recorded a song for a Disney movie, and in the same week she signed her first record contract. In 1999 she finished her first CD, *Christina Aguilera.* Soon the CD was number one in the U.S.

Over the next five years, Christina had an amazing time. She sang with Enrique Iglesias, Nelly Furtado, and Bono, from U2. She even performed for the President of the United States and toured with Justin Timberlake. She recorded a CD in Spanish, and she won a lot of music awards. She also got married!

Christina is an international superstar. She's talented and has fans of all ages, but she can't believe her success. "I simply love the job I'm doing," she says.

And what is going to happen in the future? Right now, Christina wants to continue with her singing career, but she plans to act in movies. So, you will probably see her at a movie theater near you soon.

Listening

4 🎧 **Guess the answers to the quiz. Then listen and check.**

Star quiz: Chayanne

1 Chayanne was born on June 28th, 1968 in …
  a New York.
  b Puerto Rico.
  c Madrid.

2 When he was young, he played music …
  a in church.
  b on TV.
  c on the street.

3 At the age of ten he was …
  a in a group.
  b in a movie.
  c in a TV series.

4 In 1987 he …
  a acted in some movies.
  b joined Los Chicos.
  c had an international hit.

5 Soon he was very famous and he appeared in concerts …
  a in Puerto Rico.
  b in the U.S.
  c all over the world.

6 Now Chayanne is …
  a a movie director.
  b an international superstar.
  c a TV announcer.

5 🎧 **Listen again and answer the questions.**

  1 What was Chayanne's mother's favorite TV show?
  2 What was the name of Chayanne's first group?
  3 Where was the group popular?
  4 When did Chayanne become a TV and movie actor?
  5 What was the name of Chayanne's first international hit?
  6 What did Chayanne do between 1987 and 2007?

Writing

A biography: sequencing

The first words of a sentence or paragraph sometimes help us to sequence events.

6 **Look at the text on page 98. Put the sentences in order.**

  1 d

  a **When she was young**, Christina always wanted to be a star.
  b **Christina Aguilera is now** a superstar.
  c **In 1999**, Christina finished her first CD.
  d **Christina Aguilera was born** on December 18th, 1980.
  e **Soon** the CD was number one.
  f **At the age of eight**, Christina appeared on a talent show.
  g **Over the next five years**, Christina had an amazing time.

7 **Write a biography of Chayanne. Use sequencing phrases from exercise 6 and the information from exercises 4 and 5.**

  Chayanne was born in 1968. When he was young, he …

> ● **Finished?**
>
> **Find some information about your favorite star. Write a short biography.**

Progress Check 9

Famous people

1 Match the words with pictures 1–6.

> writer businessperson singer artist
> sports star actor

Regular verbs

2 Complete the verbs with vowels *a, e, i, o,* and *u*.

1 st_p
2 pl_y
3 st_dy
4 w_rk

5 tr_v_l
6 pr_d_ct
7 d_sc_v_r
8 cr_t_c_z_

3 Write the simple past of the verbs in exercise 2.

was / were

4 Complete the sentences with *was* and *were*. Then write your answers.

Your Years Questionnaire

1 When ...... you ten years old?
2 How old ...... your mother in 2006?
3 Where ...... you on New Year's Day 2007?
4 What ...... your favorite songs last year?
5 When ...... your father born?

there was / there were

5 Choose the correct form of the verb.

There **was** / **were** an interesting movie on TV.

1 There **was** / **were** some excellent actors in it.
2 There **was** / **were** some great music.
3 There **was** / **were** some fantastic special effects.
4 There **was** / **were** a good singer in the movie.

Simple past regular verbs: affirmative and negative

6 Complete the text with the past simple of the verbs.

Madonna

Madonna Louise Veronica Ciccone was born in 1958 in the U.S. She *studied* (study) dance at university and she (**1**) ...... (start) to play music and sing when she was young. She (**2**) ...... (not finish) her studies, but she (**3**) ...... (travel) and (**4**) ...... (play) in different groups. She was soon a big pop star. In the 1980s she (**5**) ...... (act) in some movies, but the critics (**6**) ...... (not like) them. People also (**7**) ...... (criticize) her image and her videos, but that (**8**) ...... (not stop) Madonna. She now has two children, Lourdes and Rocco, and she still acts, dances, and makes good music.

10 Space

Take a look!

Find the pages where you:
- find out about the moon.
- read about Space Camp®.
- read and listen to a family's experience with a UFO.

Vocabulary

Space

1 🎧 Listen and repeat the space objects.

2 How many planets can you name?

● VOCABULARY • PAGE 129

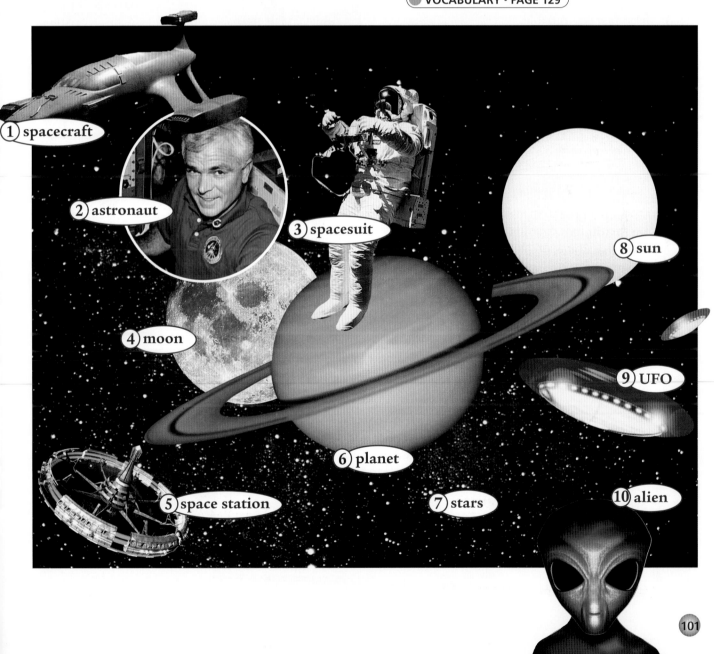

1. spacecraft
2. astronaut
3. spacesuit
4. moon
5. space station
6. planet
7. stars
8. sun
9. UFO
10. alien

101

Reading

1 🎧 **Read and listen. Put activities a–d in order.**

  a go in a spacecraft

  b meet new people

  c get up at seven o'clock

  d go to a party

2 **Read the text again. Are the sentences true or false? Correct the false sentences.**

  1 The e-mail is from Louise Walter.

  2 All of the people at the camp are from the U.S.

  3 Breakfast was terrible.

  4 Angie wore a spacesuit.

  5 She didn't go to a party.

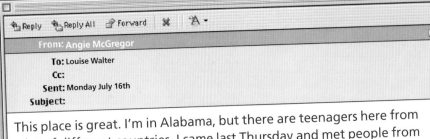

From: Angie McGregor
To: Louise Walter
Cc:
Sent: Monday July 16th
Subject:

This place is great. I'm in Alabama, but there are teenagers here from a lot of different countries. I came last Thursday and met people from Argentina, China, and India. We spoke in English, and sometimes it was very difficult.

The activities are good. We started two days ago. We got up at seven o'clock, and we had a special breakfast for astronauts. It was OK, but it was all in plastic containers. After breakfast we went to a class, and we watched a DVD about survival in space.

Yesterday was fun. I wore a spacesuit for the first time in the morning, and in the afternoon we were in a replica of a spacecraft. We looked at the computers and controls.

Last night there was a party. We didn't eat space food again; there was pizza and ice cream. I didn't go to bed until late. One of the people in my room had a video camera, and we made a science fiction movie. I acted in the movie – I think I'm going to be a movie star!

Are you having a good vacation?
Send me an e-mail with your news.

Angie

Exploring grammar

Simple past: regular and irregular verbs

3 Read the rules about regular and irregular verbs.

> The past forms of regular verbs end with **-ed**. The past forms of irregular verbs don't end with **-ed**. They have irregular forms.

4 Find the past forms of the verbs in Angie's e-mail. Copy and complete the chart.

> ~~come~~ meet speak ~~start~~ get up have go watch wear look make act

Regular	Irregular
start – *started*	come – *came*

🔘 **GRAMMAR · PAGE 124**

5 Complete the sentences with the simple past of the verbs in the box.

> go ~~make~~ wear go start make

Astronomers *made* telescopes 2,000 years ago.

1 Man first ...... into space in 1961.

2 The exploration of space ...... in 1957.

3 Laika the dog ...... into space in 1957.

4 Laika ...... a special spacesuit.

5 People ...... maps of the stars 2,000 years ago.

Time expressions: past

6 What's the date today? Write the dates for 1–4.

1 last Thursday

2 yesterday

3 two days ago

4 last night

🔘 **GRAMMAR · PAGE 124**

7 Write true and false sentences about your week. Use time expressions.

> *I went to the moon last Friday. (False)*
>
> *I got up at eight o'clock yesterday. (True)*

Speaking

8 Listen to your partner's sentences. Are they true or false?

> A: *I went to the moon last Friday.*
> B: *False!*

Vocabulary

Irregular verbs

9 🎧 Find the past forms of verbs 1–6 in the irregular verbs list. Then listen and repeat.

1	become	3	pay	5	see
2	come	4	say	6	spend

🔘 **IRREGULAR VERBS · PAGE 124**

10 Complete the text with the simple past of the verbs in exercise 9.

> In May 2001, Dennis Tito *became* the first tourist in space. Mr Tito, a 60-year-old millionaire, went into space in a Russian spacecraft and (**1**) ...... a week in the international space station. He (**2**) ...... $20m for his experience.
> In space, Dennis relaxed and listened to CDs of operas. Every day he (**3**) ...... the Earth and the stars. After his experience he (**4**) ......, "It was paradise; I just (**5**) ...... from paradise."

🔘 **Finished?**

Imagine you went into space. Write about your experiences. Then tell your partner.

I visited Pluto and I played space hockey.

Listening

1 Guess the answers to the questions.

1 When did a human first walk on the moon?
  a 1969.
  b 1929.

2 Why did people go to the moon?
  a They wanted to do scientific experiments.
  b They wanted to relax.

3 What game did the astronaut Alan Shepard play on the moon?
  a Golf.
  b Tennis.

4 Did astronauts use a car on the moon?
  a Yes, they did.
  b No, they didn't.

5 Did they find plants or water on the moon?
  a Yes, they did.
  b No, they didn't.

6 Do people go to the moon now?
  a Yes, they do.
  b No, they don't.

2 🎧 Listen to an interview with an astronaut. Check your answers.

The Space Program
This week, Ken Keane talks about the moon with astronaut Sue Forest.

Exploring grammar

Simple past: questions

3 Complete the chart with *did* and *didn't*.

Where (1)	I / you he / she / it we / you / they	go?
(2) ...... astronauts use a car on the moon?		

Short answers

Yes, they (3) .... / No, they (4) ....

(GRAMMAR • PAGE 124)

4 Put the words in order. Then answer the questions about Sue Forest.

Sue / did / When / start high school?

When did Sue start high school?
Sue started high school in 1989.

1 Where / she / did / go to high school?
2 finish high school? / When / did / she
3 did / Which university / go to? / she
4 finish university? / she / did / When
5 When / she / into space? / go / did

Space agency: personal file

Name: Sue Forest
School: Alabama High School
  1989–1993
University: Alabama University
  1994–1998
Job: astronaut
Space mission: 2006
Hobbies: golf, tennis

5 Complete the dialog with the correct forms of the verbs in the box.

relax   meet   ~~visit~~   go   like

What planet *did* you *visit*?

Neptune.

(**1**) When ...... you ...... ?

I went in December.

I played galactic soccer.

(**2**) How ...... you ...... ?

Yes, I did.

(**3**) ...... you ...... any aliens?

(**4**) And ...... you ...... the food?

No, I didn't!

6 Listen and check your answers. Then listen and repeat.

7 Write questions. Then write answers about your last vacation.

Where / go on vacation last summer?

Where did you go on vacation last summer?

I went to the beach.

1 When / go?
2 What places / visit?
3 How / relax?
4 / meet any people?
5 / like the food?
6 / go to the beach?
7 / enjoy the vacation?
8 When / come back?

Pronunciation

Word stress (2)

Three-syllable words are usually stressed on their first or second syllable.

8 Listen and repeat. Copy the chart.

vacation   teenager

9 Listen and write the words in the chart. Then listen and repeat.

1 yesterday
2 survival
3 computer
4 astronaut
5 December
6 alien

Speaking

10 In pairs, ask and answer the questions in exercise 7.

Finished?

Imagine you discovered a new planet. Draw the planet and write about it.

I discovered a new planet in August. It's called Miguelo 4. It's red and green and it has four moons. It's six billion kilometers from Earth.

Reading

1 Read the report form. Answer the questions.

When did Tom Jackson have his experience?

December 12th, 1952.

1 Where was he?
2 How many objects did he see?
3 What shape and color were they?
4 Which other people were present?

Listening

2 🎧 Listen to the first part of the interview with Victoria Jackson. What are the differences between her information and Tom Jackson's information?

3 🎧 Listen to the second part of the interview with Victoria Jackson. Which alien did she see?

 ①

 ②

 ③

TOP SECRET….TOP SECRET….TOP SECRET….TOP

Between 1947 and 1969, the United States Air Force investigated nearly 17,000 reports of UFOs. This report is typical.

TOP SECRET….TOP SECRET….TOP SECRET….TOP SECRET….TOP S

UFO REPORT

Name: Tom Jackson

Date: December 12th, 1952

Time: 9:30 p.m.

Place: Miami, Florida

Number of objects: three

Shape of objects:

Disc ☐   Boomerang ☐   Pyramid ☒   Other ☐

Color of objects: green and blue

Names of other people present: Victoria Jackson, Linda Jackson

Please describe the incident in detail:
I was at home with my wife and my daughter, Linda. We saw the objects outside the window. I shouted my wife and she scream

TOP SECRET….TOP SECRET….TOP SECRET….TOP SECRET….TOP SECRET….TOP SECRET….TOP SECRET….

Writing

A story: checking spelling

It is important to check your spelling when you write.

4 Read Alicia's story about the UFOs. Her English teacher marked the mistakes in the first paragraph. Correct the spelling of the words.

> ### Contact! by Alicia Barroso
>
> Recently I had a very strange experience. It was ~~for~~ days ago, on June 12th. I was at home ~~whit~~ my mom and dad. My dad saw the UFOs first. ~~Their~~ were three of them. They were like discs, and they were red and green.
>
> Some aliens came from one of the spaceships. They were green, and they had two eyes and big heds. One of the aliens spoke to me, but I didn't understand. I didn't run or speek. I didn't move. After four minutes the aliens went. I can't forget mi experience. It was terrible.

5 Find three mistakes in the second paragraph of Alicia's story. Correct the errors.

6 Write a story about an experience with UFOs. Think about these things:

- When did you have the experience?
- Where were you?
- Who were you with?
- Describe the UFOs.
- Describe the aliens.
- Describe your reaction and your contact with the aliens.

7 Check the spelling in your story.

Speaking

8 Read your story to the class.

⬤ Finished?

Make a spelling test for your partner. Write five correct words and five incorrect words.
teecher (**incorrect**) *astronaut* (**correct**)

Progress Check 10

Space

1 **Put the letters in order.**

uns – *sun*

1 tapnel   **3** mono   **5** ratss

2 rasatonut   **4** FOU   **6** lanie

Irregular verbs

2 **Complete the sentences with the simple past of the verbs in the box.**

come   meet   see   do   spend

Zog *saw* a fantastic space shuttle.

1 She ...... six months in space.

2 She ...... to Earth.

3 She ...... some strange creatures.

4 The creatures ...... some terrible things!

Simple past: regular and irregular verbs

3 **Correct the mistakes.**

> got
> I ~~getted~~ up at eight o'clock. I (1) hadded cereal for breakfast. Then I (2) goed to school. I (3) meeted all my friends. The English class (4) startt at nine o'clock. We (5) speaked in English and we (6) maked a poster.
>
> *Not very good. Check the spelling of the verbs!*

Time expressions: past

4 **Imagine that you are an alien. Read the questions and then write your answers.**

1 What did you have for dinner last night?

2 Where were you two days ago?

3 What did you do yesterday?

4 Where did you go last weekend?

Simple past: questions

5 **Complete the questions. Use the simple past of the verbs in parentheses. Then answer the questions.**

What *did* you *do* (do) on the weekend?

I met my friends.

1 What ...... you ...... (have) for breakfast?

2 Where ...... you ...... (go) on vacation last year?

3 What time...... you ...... (get up) yesterday?

4 ...... you ...... (study) on the weekend?

5 What ...... you ...... (eat) yesterday?

The World of English 5

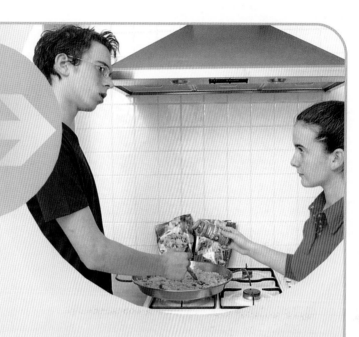

Brook Park
(pages 110 and 111)

Review: simple past

Function: Asking for clarification

1 What did Paul cook for Viki?

Culture File
(pages 112 and 113)

Topic: A visitor's view

2 What color are taxis in New York and in London?

The World of Pop (page 114)

Artist: Robbie Williams

Country: England

Song: She's the one

3 What was the name of Robbie Williams' first band?

Brook Park

I had a great time!

1

Sally What are you cooking, Paul?

Paul It's paella. It's a special meal for Viki because she's going tomorrow.

Sally Is paella a Colombian dish?

Paul Gee. I don't know.

Sally Well, it's the thought that counts.

2

Paul Well, did you like the food?

Viki It was very ... interesting, Paul. Was it a typical American dish?

Mrs. Daley No, I think it was a typical Paul dish.

Paul Well, I did my best.

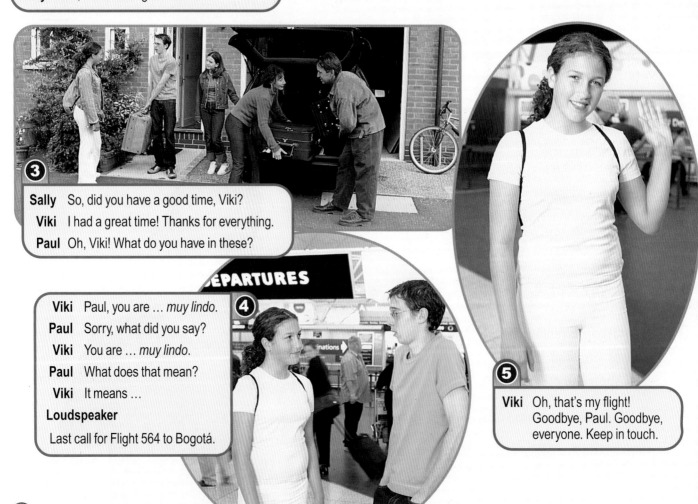

3

Sally So, did you have a good time, Viki?

Viki I had a great time! Thanks for everything.

Paul Oh, Viki! What do you have in these?

4

Viki Paul, you are ... *muy lindo*.

Paul Sorry, what did you say?

Viki You are ... *muy lindo*.

Paul What does that mean?

Viki It means ...

Loudspeaker

Last call for Flight 564 to Bogotá.

5

Viki Oh, that's my flight! Goodbye, Paul. Goodbye, everyone. Keep in touch.

Reading

1 🎧 **Read and listen to Brook Park episode 5. Then answer the questions.**

  1 Why did Paul cook for Viki?

  2 Did Viki recognize the dish?

  3 Did Viki have a good time in the U.S.?

  4 Did Paul understand Viki at the airport?

  5 Where did Viki fly to?

Useful expressions

2 **Find the expressions in the story and check their meaning.**

  1 I did my best.

  2 Did you have a good time?

  3 I had a great time!

  4 Thanks for everything.

Dialog

Clarifying meaning

3 🎧 **Look at this extract from Brook Park episode 5. Listen and repeat. Concentrate on your rhythm and intonation.**

  A: Paul, you are *muy lindo.*

  B: Sorry? What did you say?

  A: You are *muy lindo.*

  B: What does that mean?

  A: It means …

4 **Look at the useful expressions in Brook Park episodes 1 to 4. Copy an expression from each story.**

5 **In groups of three, discuss the expressions you copied in exercise 4. Use the dialog in exercise 3 as a model. Substitute the blue words to make your own dialogs.**

  A: Do me a favor.

  B: I didn't catch that. Could you repeat it?

  A: Do me a favor.

  B: What does that mean?

  A: It means …

Culture File 5

A visitor's view

1 What are your impressions of the U.S. from episodes 1–5 of Brook Park? Think about:

- the people
- the food
- what young people do

a Yes, except that young people here have more freedom. They learn to drive cars when they are sixteen, and their parents share the family car with them. Some young people drive to school. That is unusual to me. In Colombia we always take the school bus.

b Yes, I think American people are friendly. Everyone wanted to talk – especially when they discovered that I was Colombian. The sales clerks are friendly and helpful and they always say, "Have a nice day!"

e Clothes are very different here. In my country we don't often wear strange clothes. Some American people wear very big clothes, and they have lots of rings in their noses, ears, and mouths!

3 Read the interview again and answer the questions.

1 How does Viki describe Americans?

2 Do American people wear strange clothes?

3 What do many young American people do?

2 Calvin interviewed Viki for his school magazine. Match Calvin's questions 1–6 with Viki's answers a–f.

1 Do you like American people, Viki?

2 Are young people the same here?

3 What did you think of the stores?

4 What do you think of our clothes?

5 What did you think of our food?

6 Finally, what don't you like about the U.S.? Name three things!

c It was good! But there was so much of it! You can't eat it all. People eat a lot of fast food here and the portions are huge! Ice cream sundaes are my favorite.

d I didn't buy a lot because things are expensive here. I was surprised that all the stores are open on Sundays and some supermarkets are open all night.

f Hmmm. First, I don't like the weather. It rains a lot in the summer, and it's very cold and snowy in the winter. Second, the traffic in Chicago is terrible! There are a lot of cars, and the buses are always late. But really, I loved the U.S. I had a great time.

4 What do American people like eating?

5 What surprised Viki about the stores in the U.S.?

6 What things didn't Viki like?

4 What are your impressions of the U.K., from visits, movies, or books? Think about the topics in exercise 1.

5 🎧 Finn is talking about his trip to Scotland in the U.K. over summer vacation. Listen and number photos a–e in the order they are mentioned.

1d

6 🎧 Complete the sentences with the correct adjectives. Listen again and check.

1 Everything in the U.K. is ...
2 British teenagers are ...... animal rights.
3 The countryside is ...
4 British people are ...
5 The British diet is ...
6 British accents are ... to understand.

a difficult
b healthy.
c small.
d beautiful.
e interested in
f

7 C
t

P 69

The World of Pop 5

Robbie Williams

Full name: Robert Peter Maximilian Williams

Date of birth: February 13th, 1974

Place of birth: Stoke on Trent, England

Brothers and sisters: Sally

Favorite sport: soccer

First group: Take That! (1990–1995)

First solo album: *Life thru a lens* (1997)

Robbie Williams (England)

1 **Look at the information about Robbie Williams. Answer the questions.**

1 Where was Robbie born?

2 What's Robbie's sister's name?

3 How many years was Robbie in Take That!?

4 Describe Robbie's face.

2 **Complete the song with the words in the box.**

> strong   know   play   go   flying   say
> fine   free   ~~me~~

3 🎧 **Listen to the song and check your answers.**

4 **Are the sentences true or false?**

1 He loved a girl but he doesn't love her now.

2 You can be happy when you learn and you are confident.

3 The future will be difficult for the couple but they will continue.

She's the one

1 I was her, she was *me*.
2 We were one, we were (**1**) ......,
3 And if there's somebody calling me on,
4 She's the one.
5 If there's somebody calling me on,
6 She's the one.

7 We were young, we were wrong,
8 We were (**2**) ...... all along.
9 If there's somebody calling me on,
10 She's the one.

(Chorus)
11 When you get to where you wanna (**3**) ......,
12 And you know the things you wanna (**4**) ......,
13 You're smiling.
14 When you said what you wanna (**5**) ......,
15 And you know the way you wanna (**6**) ......, yeah,
16 You'll be so high you'll be (**7**) ....

17 Though the sea will be (**8**) ......,
18 I know we'll carry on,
19 'Cos if there's somebody calling me on,
20 She's the one.
21 If there's somebody calling me on,
22 She's the one.

(Repeat chorus)

Glossary

3 calling me on = helping me to go forward

8 all along = all the time

11 get to = arrive

11 wanna = want to

16 high = happy

18 carry on = continue

19 'cos = because

Grammar

Unit 1
Demonstrative pronouns

Singular
this
that

Plural
these
those

- We use *this* and *these* to talk about things that are near to us. We use *that* and *those* to talk about things that are farther away.

- We use *this* to introduce people.

  This is Nick.

be: simple present

Affirmative

Short forms		Full forms	
I	'm	I	am
you	're	you	are
he she it	's	he she it	is
we you they	're	we you they	are

Negative

Short forms		Full forms	
I	'm not	I	am not
you	aren't	you	are not
he she it	isn't	he she it	is not
we you they	aren't	we you they	are not

Questions

Am	I ...?
Are	you ...?
Is	he ...? she ...? it ...?
Are	we ...? you ...? they ...?

Short answers

Affirmative			Negative		
Yes,	I	am.	No,	I	'm not.
Yes,	you	are.	No,	you	aren't.
Yes,	he she it	is.	No,	he she it	isn't.
Yes,	we you they	are.	No,	we you they	aren't.

- We use contractions (short forms) in spoken English and in informal letters.

  Hi! My name*'s* Sarah and I*'m* twelve years old.

- We use long forms in formal letters.

Subject pronouns

Singular
I you he she it

Plural
we you they

- We use subject pronouns instead of proper nouns.

  Mary is from Canada. *She's* thirteen.

- You cannot use both the proper noun **and the subject pronoun.**

  My mother is from Mexico.

  NOT: My mother ~~she~~ is from Mexico.

- You cannot omit the subject pronoun in English.

  "Where's Tom?" "*He's* at home."

  NOT: "Where's Tom?" "~~Is~~ at home."

- We use *it* to identify people.

  "Who's that?" "*It's* John."

  NOT : "~~He's~~ John."

- **We use *it* to talk about the time, the weather, and distances.**

  It's half past three. *It*'s my birthday. *It*'s hot.
  It's 20 kilometers from here.

Interrogative pronouns

- **We use interrogative pronouns or "question words" in some questions.**

  How are you?

  How old are you?

  Who's that?

  Where's Peter now?

  What are those?

  When is your birthday?

  What time is the music club?

Unit 2

have

Affirmative	
I you	have
he she it	has
we you they	have

Negative	
I you	don't have
he she it	doesn't have
we you they	don't have

Questions		
Do	I you	have ...?
Does	he she it	have ...?
Do	we you they	have ...?

Short answers

Affirmative			Negative		
Yes,	I you	do.	No,	I you	don't.
Yes,	he she it	does.	No,	he she it	doesn't.
Yes,	we you they	do.	No,	we you they	don't.

- **We use *have* to indicate possession.**

  I *have* a computer.
  She *doesn't have* a moustache!
  How many comics *do* they *have*?

Possessive *'s*

- **After a singular noun we normally use *'s*.**
  Lucy*'s* friend is a model.

- **After a plural noun, which ends in *s*, we use an apostrophe (*'*).**
  The teachers*'* room is very nice.

Prepositions of time

- **We use *on* with days of the week and dates.**
  on Monday   *on* Tuesdays   *on* February 18th

- **We use *in* with months and years.**
  in February   *in* March   *in* 2003

- **We use *at* with times.**
  at three o'clock   *at* four-thirty

Unit 3
Simple present

Affirmative	
I you	play
he she it	plays
we you they	play

Negative	
I you	don't play
he she it	doesn't play
we you they	don't play

don't = do not
doesn't = does not

Questions

Do	I you	play?
Does	he she it	play?
Do	we you they	play?

Short answers

Affirmative			Negative		
Yes,	I you	do.	No,	I you	don't.
Yes,	he she it	does.	No,	he she it	doesn't.
Yes,	we you they	do.	No,	we you they	don't.

- **We use the simple present to talk about habits and routines.**

  We don't eat a lot of snacks.

  Do you watch TV every day?

- **We use the simple present to talk about things that are always or generally true.**

  Fruit and vegetables *contain* a lot of vitamins.

Spelling: third person singular (affirmative)

- **We form the third person singular by adding an -s to the base form.**

  play ➤ plays   like ➤ likes

- **If the verb ends in a consonant + -y, we change the -y to -i and add -es.**

  study ➤ studies

- **If the verb ends in -ch, -sh, -ss, -o or -x, we add -es.**

  watch ➤ watches
  relax ➤ relaxes
  wash ➤ washes
  go ➤ goes

Pronunciation: /ɪz/

- **When the verb ends in a consonant + -es, we pronounce the ending /ɪz/.**

  watches /ɪz/ relaxes /ɪz/ uses /ɪz/ exercises /ɪz/
  practices /ɪz/

Possessive adjectives

Subject pronouns	Possessive adjectives
I you he she it	my your his her its
we you they	our your their

Unit 4
Adverbs of frequency

- **We use adverbs of frequency to say how often an action or situation occurs.**

- **Generally, these adverbs go before the main verb.**

  My parents *usually* go to bed late.
  I *often* watch football on TV.
  NOT: ~~I watch often~~ football on TV.

Subject and object pronouns

Subject	Object
I	me
you	you
he	him
she	her
it	it
we	us
you	you
they	them

- **We always use a noun or pronoun with the verb *like*.**

  "Is football your favorite sport?"
  "Yes, I like *it* a lot."
  NOT: ~~"Yes, I like a lot."~~

Simple present: interrogative pronouns

- **Interrogative pronouns go at the beginning of questions.**

- **Remember the correct word order.**

Interrogative pronouns	do / does	Subject	Verb	Other words
Where	do	you	live?	
What time	does	the game	start	today?
What	does	Susan	watch	on TV?
How often	do	you	eat	curry?

Unit 5
Present continuous

Affirmative	
I	'm relaxing
you	're relaxing
he she it	's relaxing
we you they	're relaxing

Negative	
I	'm not relaxing
you	aren't relaxing
he she it	isn't relaxing
we you they	aren't relaxing

'm = am
're = are
's = is

'm = am
aren't = are not
isn't = is not

Questions		
Am	I	relaxing?
Are	you	relaxing?
Is	he she it	relaxing?
Are	we you they	relaxing?

Short answers					
Affirmative			Negative		
Yes,	I	am.	No,	I	'm not.
Yes,	you	are.	No,	you	aren't.
Yes,	he she it	is.	No,	he she it	isn't.
Yes,	we you they	are.	No,	we you they	aren't.

- **We use the present continuous to talk about something that is happening at the time of speaking.**

  She*'s dancing* with a police officer!

Spelling: -ing form

- **We usually form the present continuous by adding -ing to the base form.**
  sing   sing*ing*

- **If the verb ends in -e, we take off the -e and add -ing.**
  dance   danc*ing*

- **If the verb ends in a vowel + a single consonant, we double the final consonant before adding -ing.**
  stop   stop*ping*

Position of adjectives

- **Adjectives go before the noun that they are describing.**
  I don't eat *Chinese food*.
  NOT: I don't eat *food Chinese*.

- **You can use two or more adjectives together.**
  He's a *strange old* man.
  NOT: He's a man *old and strange*.

- **In sentences with the verb *be*, the adjective goes after the verb.**
  She*'s intelligent*.

Unit 6
Plurals

- **We usually form plural nouns by adding an -s to the singular form.**
  map ➤ map*s*   tent ➤ tent*s*

- **You need to add -es or -ies to form some plural nouns. These follow the same spelling rules as for the present simple (see page 117).**
  watch ➤ watch*es*
  battery ➤ batter*ies*

- **Some plural nouns are irregular.**

  person ➤ people   child ➤ children
  man ➤ men   wife ➤ wives
  woman ➤ women   knife ➤ knives

Countable and uncountable nouns

Countable	Uncountable
a motorcycle	gasoline
some motorcycles	some gasoline
six motorcycle	

- **Countable nouns have singular and plural forms.**
  battery ➤ batteries   restaurant ➤ restaurants

- **We use numbers or *a / an* with countable nouns.**
  a photo   *one* movie   *two* postcards

- **Uncountable nouns have no plural form.**
  gasoline NOT: gasolines
  water NOT: waters

- **We never use numbers or *a / an* with uncountable nouns.**
  NOT: *a* gasoline   *one* gasoline   *two* gasolines

a / an

- **We use *a / an* with singular countable nouns.**

- **We use *a* if the noun begins with a consonant.**
  There's *a* swimming pool.

- **We use *an* if the noun begins with a vowel.**
  There's *an* Internet café.
  Do you have *an* orange?

some and any

Affirmative
I have some matches.
I have some food.

Negative
I don't have any batteries.
I don't have any money.

Questions

Do you have any batteries?
Do you have any money?

- We use *some* and *any* with plural countable nouns.

- We also use *some* and *any* with uncountable nouns.

- We use *some* in affirmative sentences.
  There are *some* warm clothes in the tent.

- We use *any* in negative sentences and questions.
  You don't have *any* food.
  Are there *any* maps in the tent?

there is / there are

Affirmative

There	's is	a café.
There	are	five swimming pools.

Negative

There	isn't is not	a bank.
There	aren't are not	any cars.

Questions

Is	there	a nightclub?
Are	there	any stores?

Short answers

Affirmative	Negative
Yes, there is.	No, there isn't.
Yes, there are.	No, there aren't.

- We always use *there's* with uncountable nouns.
  There's some water here.

by and on

- **We usually use the preposition *by* with forms of transport.**
  "How do you travel to school?"
  "*By* car." / "*By* bus."
  NOT: "~~In car.~~"

- ***On foot* is the exception.**
  NOT: "~~By foot.~~"

Unit 7

can

Affirmative		Negative	
I you he she it we you they	can	I you he she it we you they	can't

can't = cannot

Questions

Can	I you he she it we you they	...?

Short answers

Affirmative			Negative		
Yes,	I you he she it we you they	can.	No,	I you he she it we you they	can't.

- After *can* we always use the base form.

  I *can make* a fire.

  NOT: ~~I can to make a fire.~~

- We use *can* to talk about ability.

  I *can* sew.

  Jim *can't* use a computer.

Pronunciation: *can*

- In affirmative sentences and questions we say /kən/.

- In negative sentences we say /kænt/.

- In affirmative short answers we say /kæn/.

should

Affirmative		Negative	
I you he she it we you they	should	I you he she it we you they	shouldn't

shouldn't = should not

- We use *should* and *shouldn't* to talk about obligation, the importance of doing or not doing something, or to give advice.

  They *should* use some insect repellent.

Imperatives

Affirmative	Negative
Stop!	Don't stop!

- We use the imperative form to give instructions and orders.

  Don't go near big rivers.

  Use a good insect repellent.

Prepositions of place

- We use *behind, on, next to, in front of, in,* and *under* to talk about the position of a thing or person.

- You do not need to use any other preposition with these phrases.

  It's behind the backpack.

  NOT: It's behind ~~of the backpack.~~

Unit 8

be going to

Affirmative		
I	'm	going to travel
you	're	going to travel
he she it	's	going to travel
we you they	're	going to travel

'm = am
're = are
's = is

Negative		
I	'm not	going to travel
you	aren't	going to travel
he she it	isn't	going to travel
we you they	aren't	going to travel

'm = am
aren't = are not
isn't = is not

Questions

Am	I	going to travel …?
Are	you	going to travel …?
Is	he she it	going to travel …?
Are	we you they	going to travel …?

- **We use** *be* + *going to* + **infinitive to talk about future plans and intentions.**

  I'm going to be a rock star.

  The tour *is going to start* in America.

Time expressions: future

- **We can use time expressions with** *next* **and** *this* **to talk about the future:**

  next Sunday / week / weekend / month / year

  this Sunday / week / weekend / month / year

  The tour is going to start *this weekend*.

- **We can also use the expressions** *tomorrow morning/afternoon/evening/night*, **and** *this evening*.

Articles: *a* / *an* and *the*

- *a* / *an* **is the indefinite article.**

- **We use** *a* / *an* **before singular countable nouns.**

- **We do not use** *a* / *an* **with plural nouns.**

  a house

  some houses

- *the* **is the definite article.**

- **We use** *the* **before singular and plural nouns.**

  The shelf is next to the table.

  The shelves are expensive.

- **In English we omit the article when we are talking about things in general.**

  Water is good for you.

  I like computer games.

  NOT: ~~I like *the* computer games.~~

Unit 9

was / were

Affirmative	
I	was
you	were
he she it	was
we you they	were

Negative	
I	wasn't
you	weren't
he she it	wasn't
we you they	weren't

wasn't = was not
weren't = were not

Questions

Was	I …?
Were	you …?
Was	he …? she …? it …?
Were	we …? you …? they …?

Short answers

Affirmative			Negative		
Yes,	I	was.	No,	I	wasn't.
Yes,	you	were.	No,	you	weren't.
Yes,	he she it	was.	No,	he she it	wasn't.
Yes,	we you they	were.	No,	we you they	weren't.

- We use *was* and *were* (the simple past forms of *be*) to talk about the state of things and people in the past.

Elvis Presley *was* a pop star.

there is / there are

Affirmative			Negative		
There	's	a person.	There	isn't	a person.
There	are	some people.	There	aren't	any people.

there was / there were

- The simple past forms of *there is* and *there are* are *there was* and *there were*.

Affirmative			Negative		
There	was	a car.	There	wasn't	a car.
There	were	some cars.	There	weren't	any cars.

wasn't = was not
weren't = were not

Questions		
Was	there	a car?
Were	there	two cars?

Short answers

Affirmative	Negative
Yes, there was.	No, there wasn't.
Yes, there were.	No, there weren't.

Simple past regular verbs

Affirmative		Negative	
I you he she it we you they	lived	I you he she it we you they	didn't live

didn't = did not

- We use the simple past to talk about states and actions in the past.

People *criticized* his work.
Some people *didn't listen*.

Spelling: simple past regular verbs

- In affirmative sentences, we usually form the simple past of regular verbs by adding *-ed* to the base form.

watch ➤ watch*ed*   play ➤ play*ed*

- If the verb ends in *-e*, we add *-d*.

live ➤ live*d*

- If the verb ends in a consonant + *-y*, we change the *-y* to *-i* before adding *-ed*.

marry ➤ marr*ied*

- If the verb ends in a vowel + a single consonant, we double the consonant before adding *-ed*.

stop ➤ stop*ped*

Pronunciation: simple past regular verbs

- When the base form of the verb ends in *-t* or *-d*, we pronounce the *-ed* ending /ɪd/.

act*ed*, visit*ed*

- When the base form of the verb ends in a vowel or a voiced consonant, we pronounce the *-ed* ending /d/.

die*d*, stay*ed*

- When the base form of the verb ends in a voiceless consonant, we pronounce the *-ed* ending /t/.

talk*ed*, danc*ed*

Unit 10
Simple past irregular verbs

- **There are some irregular verbs which do not end in -ed in the simple past form.**

  have   *had*   go   *went*

Simple past regular and irregular verbs

Questions		
Did	I you he she it we you they	find ...?

Short answers					
Affirmative			**Negative**		
Yes,	I you he she it we you they	did.	No,	I you he she it we you they	didn't.

- **We form questions in the simple past with *did* + the base form.**

  When *did* Sally *start* university?

  NOT: ~~When Sally *started* university?~~

  OR: ~~When *did* Sally *started* university?~~

Time expressions: past

- **You can use the time expressions *last ...*, and *... ago* with the simple past.**

  last night / Sunday / week / weekend / month / year

  two hours / days / weeks / months / years ago

  She started university *six months ago*.

  She started university *last year*.

Irregular verbs

Infinitive	Past simple
be /bi/	was /wəz, wɑz/, were /wər/
become /bɪ'kʌm/	became /bɪ'keɪm/
break /breɪk/	broke /broʊk/
bring /brɪŋ/	brought /brɔt/
buy /baɪ/	bought /bɔt/
can /kæn, kən/	could /kʊd, kəd/
come /kʌm/	came /keɪm/
cost /kɔst/	cost /kɔst/
do /du/	did /dɪd/
drink /drɪŋk/	drank /dræŋk/
drive /draɪv/	drove /droʊv/
eat /it/	ate /eɪt/
fall /fɔl/	fell /fɛl/
find /faɪnd/	found /faʊnd/
fly /flaɪ/	flew /flu/
forget /fər'gɛt/	forgot /fər'gɑt/
get /gɛt/	got /gɑt/
give /gɪv/	gave /geɪv/
go /goʊ/	went /wɛnt/
have /hæv/	had /hæd/
hear /hɪə(r)/	heard /hərd/
hit /hɪt/	hit /hɪt/
keep /kip/	kept /kɛpt/
know /noʊ/	knew /nu/
leave /liv/	left /lɛft/
lose /luz/	lost /lɔst/
make /meɪk/	made /meɪd/
mean /min/	meant /mɛnt/
meet /mit/	met /mɛt/
pay /peɪ/	paid /peɪd/
put /pʊt/	put /pʊt/
read /rid/	read /rɛd/
run /rʌn/	ran /ræn/
say /seɪ/	said /sɛd/
see /si/	saw /sɔ/
sell /sɛl/	sold /soʊld/
send /sɛnd/	sent /sɛnt/
sing /sɪŋ/	sang /sæŋ/
speak /spi:k/	spoke /spoʊk/
spend /spɛnd/	spent /spɛnt/
swim /swɪm/	swam /swæm/
take /teɪk/	took /tʊk/
teach /titʃ/	taught /tɔt/
tell /tɛl/	told /toʊld/
think /θɪŋk/	thought /θɔt/
throw /θroʊ/	threw /θru/
wake up /weɪk 'əp/	woke up /woʊk 'əp/
wear /wɛr/	wore /wɔr/
win /wɪn/	won /wʌn/
write /raɪt/	wrote /roʊt/

Vocabulary

Unit 1

School subjects

art /art/
calligraphy /kæ'lɪgrəfi/
English /'ɪŋglɪʃ/
French /frɛntʃ/
geography /ʤi'agrəfi/
history /'hɪstəri/
ICT /aɪsi'ti/
math /mæθ/
music /'myuzɪk/
P.E. /pi'i/
science /'saɪəns/
Spanish /'spænɪʃ/

Interests

aerobics /ɛ'roʊbɪks/
basketball /'bæskətbɔl/
chess /tʃɛs/
computer /kəm'pyutər/
environment /ɛn'vaɪərnmənt/
karate /kə'rati/
photography /fə'tagrəfi/

Countries

Africa /'æfrɪkə/
Argentina /arʤən'tinə/
Australia /ɔ'streɪlyə/
Brazil /brə'zɪl/
Britain /'brɪtn/
Japan /ʤə'pæn/
Korea /kə'rɪə/
the United Kingdom /ðə
   yunaɪtəd 'kɪŋdəm/
the United States /ðə
   yunaɪtəd 'steɪts/

Guessing the meanings of words

desert /'dɛzərt/
instrument /'ɪnstrəmənt/
kilobyte /'kɪləbaɪt/
microscope /'maɪkrəskoʊp/
mystery /'mɪstəri/
taekwondo /taɪ'kwandoʊ/
the Olympic Games /ði
   əlɪmpɪk 'geɪmz/
trumpet /'trʌmpət/

Other nouns

answer /'ænsər/
band /bænd/
beginner /bɪ'gɪnər/
best (friend) /bɛst (frɛnd)/
byte /baɪt/
capital (city) /'kæpətl ('sɪti)/

chameleon /kə'milyən/
clarinet /klærə'nɛt/
class /klæs/
classmate /'klæsmeɪt/
club /klʌb/
dragon /'drægən/
e-mail /'imeɪl/
exam /ɪg'zæm/
expert /'ɛkspərt/
flute /flut/
gym /ʤɪm/
meeting /'mitɪŋ/
movement /'muvmənt/
notice /'noʊtəs/
piano /pi'ænoʊ/
planet /'plænət/
room /rum/
saxophone /'sæksəfoʊn/
sports /spɔrts/
teacher /'titʃər/
website /'wɛbsaɪt/

Verbs

contact /'kantækt/
join /ʤɔɪn/
prefer /prɪ'fər/
send /sɛnd/

Adjectives

Brazilian /brə'zɪliən/
crazy (about) /'kreɪzi (əbaʊt)/
every (two years) /'ɛvri (tu
   'yɪrz)/
fantastic /fæn'tæstɪk/
favorite /'feɪvrət/
good (at) /gʊd (ət)/
important /ɪm'pɔrtnt/
interested (in) /'ɪntrəstəd (ɪn)/
Japanese /ʤæpən'iz/

Days of the week

Monday /'mʌndeɪ/
Tuesday /'tuzdeɪ/
Wednesday /'wɛnzdeɪ/
Thursday /'θərzdeɪ/
Friday /'fraɪdeɪ/
Saturday /'sætərdeɪ/
Sunday /'sʌndeɪ/

Months of the year

January /'ʤænyuɛri/
February /'fɛbyuəri/
March /martʃ/
April /'eɪprəl/
May /meɪ/
June /ʤun/
July /ʤʊ'laɪ/

August /'ɔgəst/
September /sɛp'tɛmbər/
October /ak'toʊbər/
November /noʊ'vɛmbər/
December /dɪ'sɛmbər/

Unit 2

Parts of the face

beard /bɪrd/
ear /ɪr/
eye /aɪ/
hair /hɛr/
moustache /'mʌstæʃ/
mouth /maʊθ/
nose /noʊz/
skin /skɪn/
teeth /tiθ/

Possessions

action figure /'ækʃn fɪgyər/
autograph /'ɔtəgræf/
bike /'baɪk/
book /bʊk/
camera /'kæmrə/
cat /kæt/
CD /si'di/
collection /kə'lɛkʃn/
comic /'kamɪk/
computer game /kəm'pyutər
   geɪm/
dog /dɔg/
DVD /divi'di/
mug /mʌg/
photo /'foʊtoʊ/
poster /'poʊstər/
watch /watʃ/

People

actor /'æktər/
actress /'æktrəs/
boyfriend /'bɔɪfrɛnd/
brother /'brʌðər/
collector /kə'lɛktər/
girlfriend /'gərlfrɛnd/
model /'madl/
monster /'manstər/
movie star /'muvi star/
sister /'sɪstər/
special effects artist /spɛʃl
   ɪ'fɛkts artɪst/
teenager /'tineɪʤər/

Other nouns

centimeter /'sɛntəmitər/
description /dɪ'skrɪpʃn/
glasses /'glæsəz/

height /haɪt/
interview /'ɪntərvyu/
magazine /'mægəzin/
meter /'mitər/
movie shoot /'muvi ʃut/
nationality /næʃə'næləti/
next (week) /nɛkst (wik)/
occupation /akyə'peɪʃn/
party /'parti/
profile /'proʊfaɪl/
screen /skrin/
theater /'θɪətər/
TV /ti'vi/

Verbs

create /kri'eɪt/
describe /dɪ'skraɪb/

Adjectives

American /ə'mɛrɪkən/
blonde /bland/
blue /blu/
brown /braʊn/
dark /dark/
famous /'feɪməs/
great /greɪt/
green /grin/
interesting /'ɪntrəstɪŋ/
long /lɔŋ/
red /rɛd/
short /ʃɔrt/
small /smɔl/
tall /tɔl/
wanted /'wantɪd/
white /waɪt/

World of English 1

Useful expressions

Do me a favor. /du mi ə
   'feɪvər/
Excuse me. /ɪk'skyuz mi/
Nice to meet you. /naɪs tə 'mit
   yu/
Wait a minute! /weɪt ə 'mɪnɪt/

Families

aunt /ænt/
brother /'brʌðər/
cousin /'kʌzn/
father /'faðər/
grandfather /'grænfaðər/
grandmother /'grænmʌðər/
grandparent /'grænpɛrənt/
mother /'mʌðər/
parent /'pɛrənt/
relative /'rɛlətɪv/

sister /ˈsɪstər/
uncle /ˈʌŋkl/

Adjectives

divorced /dəˈvɔrst/
married /ˈmærid/
related /rɪˈleɪtəd/

Unit 3
Food and drink

anchovy /ˈæntʃoʊvi/
apple /ˈæpl/
bean /bin/
bread /brɛd/
burger /ˈbərgər/
cereal /ˈsɪriəl/
chocolate /ˈtʃɑklət/
chop suey /tʃɑp ˈsui/
coffee /ˈkɔfi/
curry /ˈkʌri/
dessert /dɪˈzərt/
egg /ɛg/
fish /fɪʃ/
fruit /frut/
juice /dʒus/
meat /mit/
milk /mɪlk/
naan bread /ˈnɑrn brɛd/
nut /nʌt/
pasta /ˈpæstə/
pizza /ˈpitsə/
pork /pɔrk/
potato /pəˈteɪtoʊ/
rice /raɪs/
salad /ˈsæləd/
snack /snæk/
soup /sup/
spaghetti bolognese /spəgɛti
  boʊləˈneɪz/
tomato /təˈmeɪtoʊ/
tuna /ˈtunə/
vegetables /ˈvɛdʒtəblz/
water /ˈwɔtər/

Activities

bike /baɪk/
exercise /ˈɛksərsaɪz/
listen to music /lɪsn tə
  ˈmyuzɪk/
play an instrument /pleɪ ən
  ˈɪnstrəmənt/
play computer games /pleɪ
  kəmˈpyutər geɪmz/
relax /rɪˈlæks/
sleep /slip/

swim /swɪm/
walk /wɔk/
watch TV /wɑtʃ tiˈvi/

Other nouns

action /ˈækʃn/
body /ˈbɑdi/
brain /breɪn/
chocoholic /tʃɑkəˈhɔlɪk/
dentist /ˈdɛntɪst/
diagram /ˈdaɪəgræm/
diet /ˈdaɪət/
dislike /dɪsˈlaɪk/
elephant /ˈɛləfənt/
free time /fri ˈtaɪm/
group /grup/
habit /ˈhæbət/
heavy metal /hɛvi ˈmɛtl/
kilometer /kɪˈləmitər/
lifestyle /ˈlaɪfstaɪl/
like /laɪk/
menu /ˈmɛnyu/
mind /maɪnd/
questionnaire /kwɛstʃəˈnɛr/
restaurant /ˈrɛstrɑnt/
test /tɛst/
vegetarian /vɛdʒəˈtɛriən/
waiter /ˈweɪtər/

Verbs

control /kənˈtroʊl/
cry /kraɪ/
depend /dɪˈpɛnd/
drink /drɪŋk/
eat /it/
like /laɪk/
weigh /weɪ/

Adjectives

active /ˈæktɪv/
artistic /ɑrˈtɪstɪk/
Chinese /tʃaɪˈniz/
creative /kriˈeɪtɪv/
Scottish /ˈskɑtɪʃ/
different /ˈdɪfrənt/
healthy /ˈhɛlθi/
imaginative /ɪˈmædʒənətɪv/
Indian /ˈɪndiən/
international /ɪntərˈnæʃnl/
Italian /ɪˈtæliən/
logical /ˈlɑdʒɪkl/
mathematical /mæθˈmætɪkl/
scientific /saɪənˈtɪfɪk/
terrible /ˈtɛrəbl/
unhealthy /ʌnˈhɛlθi/

Time expressions

a (day, week, night) /ə (deɪ,
  wik, naɪt)/
every (day, week) /ˈɛvri (deɪ,
  wik)/
hour /ˈaʊər/

Linkers

and /ænd/
but /bʌt/

Unit 4
Sports

basketball /ˈbæskətbɔl/
biking /ˈbaɪkɪŋ/
bungee jumping /ˈbʌndʒi
  dʒʌmpɪŋ/
climbing /klaɪmɪŋ/
field hockey /fild ˈhɑki/
hang-gliding /ˈhæŋ glaɪdɪŋ/
ice hockey /ˈaɪs hɑki/
kayaking /ˈkaɪækɪŋ/
sailing /ˈseɪlɪŋ/
sand skiing /ˈsænd skiɪŋ/
skiing /ˈskiɪŋ/
snowboarding /ˈsnoʊbɔrdɪŋ/
soccer /sɑkər/
swimming /ˈswɪmɪŋ/
table tennis /ˈteɪbl tɛnəs/
tennis /ˈtɛnəs/
volleyball /ˈvɑlibɔl/

Daily routines

get changed /gɛt ˈtʃeɪndʒd/
get up /gɛt ˈʌp/
go to bed /goʊ tə ˈbɛd/
have breakfast /hæv ˈbrɛkfəst/
have dinner /hæv ˈdɪnər/
have lunch /hæv ˈlʌntʃ/
take a shower /teɪk ə ˈʃaʊər/
practice /ˈpræktəs/

Other nouns

activity /ækˈtɪvəti/
afternoon /æftərˈnun/
airport /ˈɛrpɔrt/
brochure /broʊˈʃʊr/
champion /ˈtʃæmpiən/
competition /kɑmpəˈtɪʃn/
distance /ˈdɪstəns/
energy /ˈɛnərdʒi/
evening /ˈivnɪŋ/
excitement /ɪkˈsaɪtmənt/
fan /fæn/
fan club /ˈfæn klʌb/

homework /ˈhoʊmwərk/
kilo /ˈkiloʊ/
limit /ˈlɪmɪt/
match /mætʃ/
million /ˈmɪlyən/
moment /ˈmoʊmənt/
newspaper /ˈnuzpeɪpər/
potato /pəˈteɪtoʊ/
practice /ˈpræktəs/
price /praɪs/
protective equipment
  /prətɛktɪv ɪˈkwɪpmənt/
receptionist /rɪˈsɛpʃnɪst/
routine /ruˈtin/
soccer player /ˈsɑkər pleɪər/
sports center /ˈspɔrts sɛntər/
star /stɑr/
team /tim/
tournament /ˈtɜrnəmənt/
truth /truθ/
U.S. /yuˈes/
weekend /wikˈɛnd/

Other verbs

beat /bit/
call /kɔl/
live /lɪv/
play /pleɪ/
prepare /prɪˈpɛr/
recommend /rɛkəˈmɛnd/
teach /titʃ/
think /θɪŋk/
travel /ˈtrævl/

Adjectives

big /bɪg/
crazy (about) /ˈkreɪzi əbaʊt/
dangerous /ˈdeɪndʒərəs/
expensive /ɪkˈspɛnsɪv/
free /fri/
future /ˈfyutʃər/
fantastic /fænˈtæstɪk/
mixed /mɪkst/
perfect /ˈpərfɪkt/
radical /ˈrædɪkl/
total /ˈtoʊtl/

Time expressions

after that /æftər ˈðæt/
finally /ˈfaɪnli/
first /fərst/
next /nɛkst/

World of English 2

Useful expressions

Do you want to go to the mall?
/du yu want tə goʊ tə θə 'mɔl/
It's a good deal /its ə gʊd 'dil/
Hey, don't be rude! /heɪ doʊnt bi 'rud/
That's not bad! /ðæts nat 'bæd/

National sports

baseball /'beɪsbɔl/
batter /'bætər/
compete /kəm'pɪt/
goal /goʊl/
goalkeeper /'goʊlkipər/
goaltender /'goʊltɛndər/
ice hockey /'aɪs haki/
league /lig/
major league /meɪdʒər 'lig/
percentage /pər'sɛntɪdʒ/
popular /papyələr/
result /rɪ'zʌlt/
run /rʌn/
scottish /'skatɪʃ/
season /'sizn/
ticket /'tɪkət/
winner /'wɪnər/
World Cup /wərld 'kʌp/
World series /wərld sɪris/

Unit 5

Celebrations

birthday /'bərθdeɪ/
carnival /'karnəvl/
Christmas /'krɪsməs/
Easter /'istər/
festival /'fɛstəvl/
Halloween /hælə'win/
Hogmanay /'hɔgməneɪ/
Mardi Gras /'mardi gra/
marriage /'mærɪdʒ/
Mass /mæs/
New Year's /nu 'yɪrz/
New Year's Eve /nu yɪrz 'iv/
Thanksgiving /θæŋks'gɪvɪŋ/
Valentine's Day /'væləntaɪnz deɪ/
wedding /'wɛdɪŋ/

Clothes

belt /bɛlt/
boot /but/
hat /hæt/

jeans /dʒinz/
skirt /skərt/
sneakers /'snikərz/
sweater /'swɛtər/
sweatshirt /'swɛtʃərt/
tracksuit /'træksut/
T-shirt /'tiʃərt/

Other nouns

Agriculture /'ægrəkʌltʃər/
bagpipes /'bægpaɪps/
candy /'kændi/
(the) Caribbean /θə kæ'rɪbiən/
cemetery /'sɛmətəri/
Christmas cake /'krɪsməs keɪk/
costume /'kastum/
date /deɪt/
drum /drʌm/
guitar /gɪ'tar/
harvest /'harvɪst/
here /hɪr/
Hindu /'hɪndu/
hundred /'hʌndrəd/
Kenya /'kɛnyə/
King cake /'kɪŋ keɪk/
man /mæn/
map /mæp/
Mexico /'mɛksɪkoʊ/
night /naɪt/
Pope /poʊp/
present /'prɛznt/
religion /rɪ'lɪdʒən/
Scotland /'skatlənd/
sofa /'soʊfə/
street /strit/
TV guide /ti'vi gaɪd/
village /'vɪlɪdʒ/
woman /'wʊmən/
world /wərld/

Other verbs

celebrate /'sɛlɪbreɪt/
dance /dæns/
do /du/
listen /'lɪsn/
make /meɪk/
pray /preɪ/
read /rid/
remember /rɪ'mɛmbər/
sing /sɪŋ/
sit /sɪt/
speak /spik/
stop /stap/
study /'stʌdi/
wear /wɛr/

work /wərk/
write /raɪt/

Adjectives

called /kɔld/
dead /dɛd/
exotic /ɪg'zatɪk/
happy /'hæpi/
traditional /trə'dɪʃnl/
typical /'tɪpɪkl/

Unit 6

The weather

cloudy /'klaʊdi/
cold /koʊld/
dry /draɪ/
hot /hat/
rainy /'reɪni/
sunny /'sʌni/
wet /wɛt/
windy /'wɪndi/

Things for a trip

backpack /bækpæk/
battery /'bætəri/
compass /'kʌmpəs/
flashlight /'flæʃlaɪt/
gasoline /gæsə'lin/
map /mæp/
match /mætʃ/
penknife /'pɛnnaɪf/
sleeping bag /'slipɪŋ bæg/
sunglasses /'sʌnglæsəz/
tent /tɛnt/
tool /tul/

Forms of transport

bike /'baɪk/
bus /bʌs/
car /kar/
helicopter /'hɛləkaptər/
motorcycle /'moʊtərsaɪkl/
plane /pleɪn/
ship /ʃɪp/
train /treɪn/

Places in the town

campground /'kæmpgraʊnd/
game arcade /'geɪm arkeɪd/
Internet café /ɪntərnɛt kæ'feɪ/
movie theater /'muvi θiətər/
nightclub /'naɪtklʌb/
sports center /'sports sɛntər/
store /stɔr/
swimming pool /'swɪmɪŋ pul/
theme park /'θim park/

Other nouns

adventure /əd'vɛntʃər/
area /'ɛriə/
banana /bə'nænə/
California /kæli'fɔrniə/
dictionary /'dɪkʃənɛri/
emergency /ɪ'mərdʒənsi/
fact /fækt/
fanatic /fə'nætɪk/
hot dog /'hat dɔg/
luck /lʌk/
lunchtime /'lʌntʃtaɪm/
money /'mʌni/
mosquito /məs'kitoʊ/
paper /'peɪpər/
person (people) /'pərsn ('pipl)/
postcard /'poʊstkard/
preparation /prɛpə'reɪʃn/
problem /'prabləm/
program /'proʊgræm/
route /rut/
survey /'sərveɪ/
teddy bear /'tɛdi bɛr/
temperature /'tɛmprətʃər/
traffic /'træfɪk/
traveler /'trævlər/
trip /trɪp/

Verbs

cross /krɔs/
explain /ɪk'spleɪn/
find /faɪnd/
finish /'fɪnɪʃ/
hate /heɪt/
look for /'lʊk fər/
need /nid/
plan /plæn/
see /si/
share /ʃɛr/
take /teɪk/
visit /'vɪzət/

Adjectives

basic /'beɪsɪk/
excellent /'ɛksələnt/
extra /'ɛkstrə/
near /nɪr/
warm /wɔrm/

Writing a letter

Dear /dɪr/
Sincerely /sɪn'sɪrli/

Adverb

obviously /'abviəsli/

Vocabulary 127

World of English 3

Useful expressions

Are you having fun? /ɑr yu ˈhævɪŋ fʌn/
I'm impressed. /aɪm ɪmˈprɛst/
Me too. /mi ˈtu/
You're joking. /yɔr ˈdʒoukɪŋ/

Clubs for young people

badge /bædʒ/
boy scout /bɔɪ ˈskaʊt/
camp /kæmp/
climbing /ˈklaɪmɪŋ/
cook /kʊk/
cub scout /kʌb ˈskaʊt/
earn /ɜrn/
first aid /fɜrst ˈeɪd/
fishing /ˈfɪʃɪŋ/
kayaking /ˈkaɪækɪŋ/
leader /ˈlidər/
member /ˈmɛmbər/
merit /ˈmɛrət/
organization /ɔrgənəˈzeɪʃn/
outdoor /ˈaʊtdər/
patrol /pəˈtroʊl/
rank /ræŋk/
scoutmaster /ˈskaʊtmæstər/
skill /skɪl/
survival /sərˈvaɪvl/
troop /trup/
youth /yuθ/

Unit 7

Animals

(emperor) penguin /(ˈɛmpərər) ˈpɛŋgwən/
(sea) eagle /(si) ˈigl/
butterfly /ˈbʌtərflaɪ/
camel /ˈkæml/
chameleon /kəˈmilyən/
crocodile /ˈkrɑkədaɪl/
fish /fɪʃ/
frog /frɔg/
monkey /ˈmʌŋki/
mosquito /məˈskitoʊ/
mouse /maʊs/
parrot /ˈpærət/
polar bear /poʊlə ˈbɛr/
rat /ræt/
scorpion /ˈskɔrpiən/
snake /sneɪk/
spider /ˈspaɪdər/
taipan /taɪˈpæn/

Other nouns

Aborigine /æbəˈrɪdʒəni/
Antarctic /ænˈtɑrktɪk/
blood /blʌd/
camouflage /ˈkæməflɑʒ/
CD player /si ˈdi pleɪər/
cell phone /ˈsɛl foʊn/
centigrade /ˈsɛntɪgreɪd/
coast /koʊst/
community /kəˈmyunəti/
danger /ˈdeɪndʒər/
didgeridoo /dɪdʒəriˈdu/
disease /dɪˈziz/
encyclopaedia /ɛnsaɪkləˈpidiə/
environment /ɛnˈvaɪrənmənt/
glass /glæs/
habitat /ˈhæbətæt/
human /ˈhyumən/
insect repellent /ˈɪnsɛkt rɪpɛlənt/
Internet /ˈɪntərnɛt/
jungle /ˈdʒʌŋgl/
knife /naɪf/
knowledge /ˈnɑlɪdʒ/
liquid /ˈlɪkwɪd/
minimum /ˈmɪnəməm/
minute /ˈmɪnət/
object /ˈɑbdʒɛkt/
plant /plɑnt/
predator /ˈprɛdətər/
protection /prəˈtɛkʃn/
river /ˈrɪvər/
shelter /ˈʃɛltər/
size /saɪz/
survival /sərˈvaɪvl/
weight /weɪt/

Skills

adapt /əˈdæpt/
cook /kʊk/
hunt /hʌnt/
look for /ˈlʊk fɔr/
make a fire /meɪk ə ˈfaɪər/
play an instrument /pleɪ ən ˈɪnstrəmənt/
run /rʌn/
sew /soʊ/
speak a language /spik ə ˈlæŋgwɪdʒ/
survive /sərˈvaɪv/
use a computer /yuz ə kəmˈpyutər/

Other verbs

conserve /kənˈsərv/
escape /ɪˈskeɪp/
fly /flaɪ/
go in /goʊ ˈɪn/
imitate /ˈɪməteɪt/
need /nid/
panic /ˈpænɪk/
protect /prəˈtɛkt/
smoke /smoʊk/
stay /steɪ/
sterilize /ˈstɛrəlaɪz/
touch /tʌtʃ/
use /yuz/

Adjectives

careful /(bi) ˈkɛrfl/
common /ˈkɑmən/
contaminated /kənˈtæməneɪtɪd/
dark /dɑrk/
domestic /dəˈmɛstɪk/
extreme /ɪkˈstrim/
French /frɛntʃ/
minus /ˈmaɪnəs/
natural /ˈnætʃərəl/
poisonous /ˈpɔɪznəs/
strange /streɪndʒ/
wild /waɪld/

Prepositions of place

behind /bɪˈhaɪnd/
in /ɪn/
in front of /ɪn ˈfrʌnt əv/
next to /ˈnɛks tu/
on /ɑn/
under /ˈʌndər/

Adverbs

efficiently /ɪˈfɪʃntli/
particularly /pərˈtɪkyələrli/
without /wɪˈðaʊt/

Unit 8

Furniture

bed /bɛd/
bedside table /bɛdsaɪd ˈteɪbl/
closet /ˈklɑsət/
cupboard /ˈkʌbərd/
desk /dɛsk/
lamp /læmp/
light /laɪt/
mirror /ˈmɪrər/
shelf /ʃɛlf/
stereo /ˈstɛrioʊ/

A house

attic /ˈætɪk/
bathroom /ˈbæθrum/
bedroom /ˈbɛdrum/
hallway /ˈhɔlweɪ/
kitchen /ˈkɪtʃɪn/
living room /ˈlɪvɪŋ rum/
stairway /ˈstɛrweɪ/
study /ˈstʌdi/
wall /wɔl/
yard /yard/

Other nouns

plane /pleɪn/
car racing /ˈkɑr reɪsɪŋ/
cause /kɔz/
cello /ˈtʃɛloʊ/
door /dɔr/
home /hoʊm/
idea /aɪˈdɪə/
look /lʊk/
millionaire /mɪlyəˈnɛr/
neighbor /ˈneɪbər/
plan /plæn/
practice /ˈpræktəs/
reason /ˈrizn/
reptile /ˈrɛptaɪl/
string /strɪŋ/
violin /vaɪəˈlɪn/
winner /ˈwɪnər/

Verbs

avoid /əˈvɔɪd/
buy /baɪ/
change /tʃeɪndʒ/
decorate /ˈdɛkəreɪt/
have a party /hæv ə ˈparti/
invite /ɪnˈvaɪt/
learn /lərn/
move /muv/
paint /peɪnt/
review /rɪˈvyu/
suppose /səˈpoʊz/
want /wɑnt/

Adjectives

excellent /ˈɛksələnt/
expensive /ɪkˈspɛnsɪv/
fun /fʌn/
light green /laɪt ˈgrin/
new /nu/
nice /naɪs/
violent /ˈvaɪələnt/
yellow /yɛloʊ/